Elmer Kintner Jr.

3.10

W9-AOB-596

THE DIVINE PURPOSE IN US

F. Henry Edwards

The Divine
Purpose in Us

Herald Publishing House, Independence, Missouri

Preface

The Divine Purpose in Us first appeared as a set of quarterlies which were published in 1937 and 1938. These quarterlies have been out of print for several years, although closely related material was included in some of my later books, notably *Authority and Spiritual Power* (1956).

Some months ago Elders Clifford P. Buck and Richard B. Lancaster of the Department of Religious Education asked that I prepare the remainder of the quarterly material for republication. I was hard pressed for time, and Brother Lancaster volunteered to make a preliminary revision of the section to be included so as to bring the work up to date. He did this very painstakingly, giving many hours to the work, and for his able and conscientious help I am deeply grateful.

I have now gone over the entire manuscript, rewriting many sections and adding several chapters, and I present it to those who may be interested with the earnest prayer that God will use it as a means of furthering his purpose in many lives.

F. HENRY EDWARDS

Acknowledgments

In preparing this manuscript I drew on the quarterly, *The Divine Purpose in Us,* and repeated the references used there although they are now rather old and several of the books used are not readily available. However, the revision has required extensive additional reading and I have given these references as they have occurred in the text.

Mrs. Jean Spiller and Mrs. Bertha Steck of the office of the First Presidency have given consistent and pleasant and valuable help, which I am happy to acknowledge.

My wife, Alice, made a major contribution to the style of the quarterlies, and she reviewed and corrected this manuscript with diligent care. Here, as on many other points, my ministry has been greatly enriched by her affection and insight and skill.

F. HENRY EDWARDS

Contents

Part I

The Unfolding Purpose

1 | What Is Man?

WE ARE SEEKING TO discover whether there is meaning and purpose to life and, if so, what this meaning and purpose is. As we are about to start our inquiry it will be well to look at ourselves and to observe the kind of persons we are. Our first question is "What is man?"

Without undue diffidence or egotism, we may echo the word of the greatest of English poets:

> What a piece of work is a man!
> How noble in reason! How infinite in faculty!
> In form and moving how express and admirable!
> In action how like an angel!
> In apprehension how like a god!
> The beauty of the world!
> The paragon of animals![1]

We are here, in the midst of the eternities, endowed with many gifts, "fearfully and wonderfully made," and seeking to exercise an expanding dominion over all that we see and know. But the obvious facts of our history also tell us that there is another side to man's nature that threatens his very existence. It was these dark and tragic depths that caused the same poet to write: "Life is a tale told by an idiot full of sound and fury, signifying nothing."

As Christian people we believe that though we are creatures of the dust, yet we are fashioned after the likeness of Divinity — God created man in his own image.[2] He formed the spirit of man within us.[3] As Paul says, "In him we live, and move, and have our being . . . for we are also his offspring."[4]

From the physical point of view it is quite clear that man is biologically an animal. Let us not resent this, or think that by denial we can change the facts. In and of itself there is no need to deny it, since religion must deal with the whole man. Because man's physical structure shows him to be one of the higher vertebrates many things which we have learned about the bodily functions of animals can be used to promote our own health and vigor. It is part of God's plan. Let us recognize and be grateful for this. But this does not mean that we should study man as if he were no more than a highly complex animal and an intriguing illustration of the working of physical laws. Much contemporary writing does this, treating man as though he were merely a bundle of biological and psychological impulses. When we do this, truth is distorted in that fact is taken for the whole.

The fact that we are related to the animals is not the most important truth about man. The note struck in the first chapter of Genesis and resounding throughout scripture is surely sounder and truer. "Man is spirit"[5] and "there is a spirit in man."[6] We are related to God. "Man is the tabernacle of God, even temples."[7] We are of the earth, earthy; but we are also of the heavens, heavenly; consequently we cannot live by bread alone, but need also the spiritual food which our heavenly Father provides daily.

We are strange creatures in many ways, but strangest of all in that we alone among all the animals are forever in revolt against being just animals. More important than our relationship to the lower orders of creation is our difference

11

from them. We struggle constantly from beastliness to god-liness. The animal within urges us to remain content with our possessions in the satisfaction of our appetites. But the God within will not let us be content. We know the meaning of honor even though we are not always honorable. We see the beauty of courage even though we are frequently coward-ly. We hear the voice of beauty even though we do not always obey.

The prophets and seers have all been keenly aware of our dual personality, and of the eternal conflict between the "inner man" and the "outward man."[8] We know the strength of temptations downward, but we also know the attraction of temptations upward. We have not been left alone, the prey of our carnal natures; all around us are inducements to righteousness. And, what is more, as we respond to the best that we know we come to feel an inner assurance that we can continue to respond. So may we in time learn to make the lesser parts of our natures the servants of the greater.

DOMINION AND DESTINY

The Psalmist asks, "What is man, that thou art mindful of him? and the son of man, that thou visitest him?" Then he answers his own deep questions, "Thou hast made him a little lower than the angels, and hast crowned him with glory and honor. Thou madest him to have dominion over the works of thy hands."[9] The word "dominion" which is used here is one of the key words of our history. In response to the command of God noted here and written into our nature from the beginning,[10] our story has been one of expanding conquest. We are not content to enjoy the flowers and fruits and to domesticate the useful animals, but have improved the quality of many other living things. By careful selection and crossing we have produced the shasta from the common daisy, the tea rose from the hedge flower, the sturdy nasturtium from its frail progenitor. Under our guidance the common grasses have come to yield the golden grain upon which man and beast subsist. Not only have we improved the quality of the peach and the plum, but they have been combined to bring into being the priceless nectarine.

The wild horses of the plain have become the ancestors of Belgian draught horses and of the fleetest racer. We have bred Holstein cows for quantity and Jerseys for quality of milk and then mated them to produce the new Holstein giving both quantity and quality. Even the much abused mule — though lacking pride of ancestry or hope of posterity — combines the intelligence of the horse and the sagacity and endurance of the donkey. In endeavors such as these dominion has come to the very edge of partnership in creation.

None of this has been achieved by the driving force of blind chance. We are creatures of intelligence, exploring the wilderness and making highways across the deserts. Intelligence and self-discipline have pointed the way, and earth and sea and air are gradually yielding their treasures and submitting to our will. We who can read the secrets in the heart of the atom and weigh the stars in their courses surely belong to a higher order of life than either atoms or stars. Mass is not the true measure of what is consequential in the universe, nor is force the final standard. We ourselves hold the key. The stupendously significant fact of the universe is that man *is* and that we are on the way to greatness, called by a destiny greater than we yet know.

MAN'S DESPERATE NEED

Yet the pride which lifts its head when we contemplate the achievements of our race is humbled by two unquestioned facts: such power as we have is borrowed, and it has not yet extended over our own lives. We do not create or set in motion the laws of life; we only discover and use them. They belong to God. And we have not yet learned to submit to them ourselves in the interest of our own larger life.

Indeed, we want our own way and are in rebellion against the disciplines of the larger life. This rebellion has continued so long that it has become habitual and is part of our very nature. We are stubbornly selfish, quick to see our own immediate advantage, and slow to share with each other. When we would do good, the evil habits of the yesterdays still remain as part of ourselves and impede our achievement of good.[11] We are lost until we receive the promised blessing: "A new heart also will I give you, and a new spirit will I put within you; and I will take away the stony heart out of your flesh, and I will give you a heart of flesh. And I will put my Spirit within you, and cause you to walk in my statutes, and ye shall keep my judgments, and do them."[12]

Our very greatness brings us to the point of desperate need. If we were "finished and finite clods, untroubled by a spark"[13] there would be no problem. If we were creatures of light, untempted by things that are tawdry and cheap, there would be no problem. But we are neither of these. We are "a little lower than the angels"[14] and though our inner man has heard the music of eternity, "through fear of death" all during our lifetime, we are "subject to bondage."[15] We dream and plan and work, but our greatest dreams must be left for our children and grandchildren to complete. This too humbles us. We cannot command life, but are completely dependent on God for such life as we borrow. In very truth, it is "in him we live, and move, and have our being."[16]

If, then, we are to find meaning and purpose in life, we must face the facts of our creation as we know them to be. We must see ourselves as men, built for dominion, and yet lacking dominion over ourselves. We are people of destiny, but this destiny is finally in the hands of God. The great claim that man is created in the image of God means that we must face God if we are to understand human life. Man is not a "thing," though his body obeys the laws of biological organisms. Man is so created that his essential kinships are with things above him and not merely with that which is below him. The way to strength and power and life is the way of resolute and intelligent endeavor carried forward in the spirit of reverence and humility in obedience to the voice of God.

---

1. Shakespeare, *Hamlet,* Act II.
2. Gen. 1:26, 27; D. and C. 17:4.
3. Zech. 12:1.
4. Acts 17:28.
5. D. and C. 90:5 d.
6. Job 32:8; see also I Cor. 2:11.
7. D. and C. 90:5 f.
8. II Cor. 4:16.
9. Ps. 8:4-6.
10. Gen. 1:25-30.
11. Rom. 7:19-24.
12. Ezek. 36:26, 27.
13. Browning, "Rabbi Ben Ezra"
14. Ps. 8:5.
15. Heb. 2:15.
16. Acts 17:28.

2 | Life Is Purposeful

WE ARE LIVING in a world of challenge and opportunity. The good and the bad, the superior and the trivial, compete for our attention. It is our task to choose a path among the diverse demands of life. Suppose we were all compelled to declare truthfully what our purpose in life is, what would our answers be? "to earn a living"? "to be popular"? "to wield great power"? "to have a good time"? "to do my duty"? "to save my soul"? "to help build the kingdom of God"?

These might be some of the answers that would be given. But it is quite likely that many persons would not be able to give any definite answer. For others, their verbal answer would not really reflect their true purpose. Some persons just live on from day to day, swayed by many appeals, trying to get along, having a pleasant time without flagrantly violating the accepted codes of conduct. The picture painted by Matthew Arnold, though pessimistic, is not untrue:

> Most men eddy about
> Here and there — eat and drink,
> Chatter and love and hate,
> Gather and squander, are raised
> Aloft, are hurled in the dust,
> Striving blindly, achieving
> Nothing.[1]

Caught in the backlash of two great wars, living on the brink of world disaster, mankind has a great stake in the clarity with which we see our need for the guidance of religious faith. This faith must answer the question, "Is there any abiding purpose in life?"

MAN IN GOD'S PURPOSE

Among all the peoples of antiquity probably none have made such an impact upon the course of history as the Hebrews. Many other ancient nations are forgotten by all except historians and archaeologists, but the people of ancient Israel are not forgotten. The miracle of their survival as a people is a phenomenon of history. The extent of the impact of their life and literature is incalculable; they knew that life is purposeful; they had a sense of destiny. This is the key to their greatness.

The book of Genesis does not begin with idle fables explaining in detail how this world came into being, as many ancient mythologies of other cultures do; it is an account which in all spiritual aspects is forever true. Among its great affirmations are these: (1) God created all things; life is not a cosmic accident; (2) all things in their true nature and use are "very good"; (3) man was designed for eternal fellowship; (4) the real misery of man comes from his disobedience and rebellion; and (5) even in his fallen state man is not beyond the providence of the good God who made him, and who is slowly working out His righteous and loving purpose in him.

Other ancient mythologies portray gods of caprice and whim. Their actions are controlled by all too human emotions — jealousy, lust, anger. Creation itself is thought to be without any profound purpose, more or less an afterthought of the gods, in Babylonian and Egyptian stories of the beginning. In striking contrast, the God revealed in Genesis is a God of profound purpose and consistent law. His every act in creation was designed to a certain end. The purposes of the God of the Hebrews are seen as never changing; he is consistent in all his actions and in all his demands upon man. The revelation of his intention in creating man and his relationship to man is characterized by deep dignity and abiding meaning.

REVELATION AND SCIENCE AGREE

It may seem a far cry from the story of the beginnings of life as told in the book of Genesis to the story being written today by men of science — geologists, astronomers, biologists, physicists. But is it? The conflict is not as great as it is sometimes made to appear. Scientists have one conviction in common, that nothing happens without cause. They believe that all life is linked together in an infinite chain, and that there is reason everywhere. There are scientific events that testify to a universe of cause and effect; it is only logical to believe in a great cause behind all others.

The idea of progress which is so dear to the hearts of modern people involves the idea of purpose. There is no such thing as progress by blind chance, for progress means approach toward a goal, and we do not achieve important goals by accident. Life has goals, and people who really live approach these goals. We are not satisfied merely with the thought that the universe is a "going concern." Something within ourselves demands that it shall be going somewhere. That is why we can always find newspaper space for predictions regarding the end of the world, whether those predictions place the event millions of years in the future, or this afternoon! It is important for us to know if life shall sometime cease for all men; for if it does, and the future holds nothing but blankness, then the beauty and purpose and significance and drive is taken out of life for today and for every day.

The importance of a sense of purpose is illustrated and illuminated in the account of a conversation between Dr. W. E. Hocking and a friend. Dr. Hocking writes:

A short time ago as I was talking with a colleague, a psychiatrist, he said, "Something has been occurring to me recently which seems important, and yet it is so simple that I can hardly believe it very significant. It is a way of taking the miscellany of events which make up the day's impressions of the world. One sees no trend in them. But suppose there were a trend which we cannot define but can nevertheless have an inkling of. There is certainly some direction in evolution, why not in history? If there were such a trend, then we men could be either with it or against it. To be with it would give a certain peace and settlement; to be against it would involve a subtle inner restlessness. To have confidence in it would be a sort of commitment, for better or for worse. I wonder if that is what you mean by religion."

"Yes," I said.

"Well, is that all there is to it?"

"I think that is the substance of it. The great religious ones seem to have had a certainty that they were going along with the trend of the world. They have had a passion for right living which they conceived of as a cosmic demand."

"There is nothing contrary to science in that."

"No, but it makes a difference, doesn't it?"

"Strange that such a simple thing should make so very much difference."[2]

POWERS OF LIFE RELEASED

One of the things which differentiates men from the lesser animals is the ability to anticipate and plan for a complex future. Man has been called "the creature with a forehead." The brain development of the prefrontal region is the basis for a rational life beyond new sense impressions and reflex reactions. Much as we are amazed at the ability of the arctic tern to fly from the North Pole to the South Pole by instinct, we value the power to reason above even that. Although some animals work in the summer to provide the needs of life for the winter, nowhere is the power of anticipation so keen, so acute, and so diverse as in men. Indeed, we regard careful anticipation of future needs and possibilities as one of the characteristics of worthwhile people, and tend to despise those who live a butterfly existence from day to day without thought of tomorrow. Here then is a social testimony to the importance of purpose. Life should be definitely pointed toward goals which gather up our lesser strivings and redeem them from waywardness.

A controlling purpose does actually release the powers of life. Taken by itself, the business of learning the organs and functions of the human body is a staggering task. But when viewed as a means to becoming a doctor, and thus serving one's community honorably and responsibly, this task is not nearly so arduous. This is not imagination. It is a demonstrable fact. Many a man who could not find the time nor the strength to walk a couple of miles for the sake of walking will find pleasure and health in hitting a little ball across the green meadows, following it carefully, searching for it in hidden places, and hitting it again, with the crazy but fascinating purpose of seeing in how few strokes he can send that ball into the nine or eighteen holes of his favorite golf course.

One of the most important contributions made to our lives by achievement of a noble and inclusive purpose is release from the oppression of passing circumstance. What a tremendous amount of energy is consumed in resentment and fear by the person who lives from day to day without the consolation and encouragement of the larger vision. And how much of this useless dissipation of power is eliminated by the man whose vision of the distant goal reduces the hills and valleys of the immediate present to something approaching their proper proportions. Lincoln had no time to resent the slights put on him by General McClellan. If necessary, he was willing to hold the general's horse, asking only one thing — that the cause of the Union should be advanced.

Without question, a great purpose provides the incentive for the control of habit. So many people are the captives of their own appetites. They spend money that they cannot spare for tobacco and strong drinks, waste life and health in unsatisfying dissipation, and fall short of greatness because of their engrossment with trivialities. Sensing something of their situation, well-meaning persons in this category concentrate on giving up tobacco, or strong drinks, or habits of uncleanliness, but all too frequently they fall back defeated into the habits from which they sought escape. This is because even negative concentration on a habit tends to confirm it. We think about fasting and immediately become hungry. We think of temperance and immediately become thirsty. But concentration on a greater purpose takes care of these lesser problems in passing. We may be too busy to eat, or may become too engrossed in some worthwhile hobby to take time for dissipation.

Best of all, when we become enlisted in a great cause we become passionately devoted to its success. We feel that some significant measure of responsibility for that success rests on us. Without counting the cost we give gladly for the cause's sake, and find manhood in so doing. At one time a young man came to Whistler, the artist, with a new and beautiful picture to hang. He wanted help from Whistler because the picture did not seem to fit the room. The great artist, after looking over the matter said, "Man, you're beginning at the wrong end. You can't make the painting fit the room. You will have to make the room fit the painting." So it is with great causes; we are remade to fit our highest allegiances.

LIFE'S ULTIMATE ALLEGIANCE

Singleness of purpose is vital to the successful life. You cannot dissipate your powers and still win. At first it almost seems that it does not matter what the object of your worship might be. The joy of the miser who runs his gold through his fingers for the sheer delight of feeling and hearing it; the joy of the lover whose world becomes radiant when his beloved smiles; the joy of the artist who brings color and form and beauty to life as the dying sun reaches into his empty attic; the joy of the bookworm who knows each volume by name and dusts and caresses and loves it — all these are the joys of the man who has found a single purpose that to him is supremely worthwhile. He has found a god, even though it is false, and he has surrendered himself to its service.

But the trouble with the worship of these lesser gods is that the more ardent the worshiper the narrower his life becomes; the miser lives for his money, or the artist "for art's sake" and no one else can talk his language. Then the rest of his nature begins to protest. Some unsatisfied part of life rises up and demands attention. To paraphrase Lincoln, "He can fool part of his nature all of the time and all of his nature part of the time, but he cannot fool all of his nature all of the time." If a man's one great interest is not big enough and true enough, some occasion will come when the best part of him will rebel against being forgotten or against being enlisted under the banner of some triviality. The only real satisfaction is to worship a God who satisfies our nature at all points. This demands the worship of the only true God, who calls us to direct every aspect of our lives toward him and who, as we do worship him, gives us satisfaction in every part of life. That is the reason for the ancient law:

> Thou shalt have no other gods before me. Thou shalt not make unto thee any graven image, or any likeness of any thing that is in heaven above, or that is in the earth beneath, or that is in the water under the earth; thou shalt not bow down thyself to them, nor serve them.[3]

It is also the lesson which Jesus sought to teach when he said:

22

Where your treasure is, there will your heart be also. The light of the body is the eye; if therefore thine eye be single to the glory of God, thy whole body shall be full of light. But if thine eye be evil, thy whole body shall be full of darkness. If therefore the light which is in thee be darkness, how great shall that darkness be.[4]

Life is purposeful, and the only purpose which finally matters is the inclusive purpose which Christianity sets before us. God has revealed himself as committed to man. The extent of his concern for man is the heart of the New Testament story. As we shall see, it is ultimately in Christ that life takes on enduring purpose and meaning.

Against this background it is small wonder that a man of the caliber of Harry Emerson Fosdick writes,

Life cannot go on without spiritual meaning. We can go on without automobiles and airplanes. We can live on a dollar a day if we have to, but if life has no aims, no directions, no purpose, if there is no essential and abiding meaning in it, then it is dust and ashes to our taste.[5]

1. Matthew Arnold, "Rugby Chapel."
2. William Ernest Hocking, *What Man Can Make of Man,* New York: Harper and Bros., pp. 60-61.
3. Exod. 20:3-5.
4. Matt. 6:21-23.
5. Harry Emerson Fosdick, *The Secret of Victorious Living.*

3 | The Glory of God

TWO MAJOR PICTURES of the universe are possible. The first depicts it as a realm of chance and accident. From this viewpoint natural law seems to govern, but none of the ultimate and important things are guaranteed. Life may vanish into nothingness at any time. Levin in Tolstoy's *Anna Karenina* betrays the agony of one led astray by this philosophy. "Without knowing what I am and why I am here," he agonizes, "life is impossible. In infinite time, in infinite matter, in infinite space, is formed a bubble-organism, and that bubble lasts awhile and bursts, and that bubble is me!" Life taught him in time that this interpretation of life "was an agonizing error."[1]

Another point of view is that a Power higher than ourselves has a hold upon men, and is constantly endeavoring to break into our lives. From this viewpoint the universe is in the hand of God and moves toward the accomplishment of his purpose. This is the Christian conviction.

FASHIONED IN LOVE

One of the fundamental affirmations of Christianity is that we did not come here of our own volition, but as the direct result of the creative act of God. It does not greatly matter whether we believe that man's creation took place in a moment of time or whether it was achieved in the long process of evolution. Whatever the method used, we are confronted with the original facts: the fact of God and of his creative acts.

A creator sufficiently wise and able to bring our world order into being, to place us here on earth, and to make available those forces by which life is sustained would not do all this without some purpose. To think other than this is to charge Divinity with the most rank foolishness. There is a purpose to our life, a reason behind our creation. And this purpose, this reason, is not primarily ours; it is God's. Our purpose in life does not originate in ourselves but in Divinity creating us. If "God is love,"[2] God's purposes must be an expression of love.

From the beginning, men of keen spiritual vision have sensed this fact, but its true significance is not realized until we get the essentially Christian point of view. Christianity affirms that Christ Jesus our Lord was the active agent in creation. Because we know that our Lord loves us we know that creation is permeated with this affection for us, and Paul's statement to the Colossian saints becomes a paean of praise:

> By him were all things created, that are in heaven, and that are in earth, visible and invisible, whether they be thrones, or dominions, or principalities, or powers; all things were created by him, and for him.[3]

ENVELOPING POWER AND PURPOSE

We are set to work out our destiny, then, in a world which has been fashioned in love. But that is not all. At every step of the way we are dependent upon forces greater than we are, and our achievement rests upon our cooperation with these forces. All that we have to do is to learn to take advantage of the opportunities of life. We are channels through whom life flows. We originate nothing. The nurse spanks the newborn baby. It cries. Air rushes into the lungs, and life has begun. But neither the baby nor the nurse made

25

the air act that way. Each of us adapts ourselves to the air, or we die. In much the same way the great scientist goes to his laboratory. He remembers things which have been discovered by other thinkers, and uses apparatus which has been devised by other inventors, and by these means sets himself to watch nature at her task. One scientist in ten thousand perceives some new truth and is acclaimed by the multitude. But what really happens? No one can be sure. The nearest that we can say is that the scientist puts himself into a condition of receptivity, and understanding rushes in on him. He does not make the truth he discovers. He cannot say how it comes. The last step toward the light is a step of pure inspiration.

Perception of scientific truth crowds into the mind of the scientist when conditions are favorable, just as the air rushes into the baby's lungs. But the scientist is not the only factor in the situation. Truth was already built into the structure of life. It was not just awaiting discovery. Every other truth was pointing to it. There is something outside and above this visible world; and the further we get from mundane things the more sure we are that this higher and enveloping power which constantly breaks in on our senses is of God.

It is a perception of this enveloping purpose, combined with the growing conviction that love is at the heart of it, which has inspired men of vision in every generation. Once we really feel that creation is purposeful and that the aim running through it is the loving purpose of our heavenly Father we become eager to make his intention our own and to cooperate as fully as possible with his plans for us. We cease to be rebellious. We realize that he is more loyal to our highest aspirations than we are. However exalted our own ideals for ourselves and for society may be, we realize that they are surpassed by the purpose of God for us.

The fullness of his purpose is greater than we can yet

imagine, for "eye hath not seen, nor ear heard, neither have entered into the heart of man, the things which God hath prepared for them that love him."[4] His purpose for us is that we shall attain to immortality and eternal life and enjoy full and unrestricted communion with him in "the church of the Firstborn."[5] It takes time to achieve such a purpose, but only such a purpose can satisfy our deep-laid craving for Divinity. H. G. Wells has phrased this for us:

> We are here, my brothers, for what end? To serve the purpose and the spirit that has been breathed into our lives. We live not for ourselves, but for growth, growth that goes on forever. To grow out of our cracks and crannies, out of our meanness and littleness, out of our blindness and darkness into greatness and light. To grow, at last, into the understanding of God.

Both in the natural world and in the spiritual world the greatest glory of any created thing is that it shall fully serve the purpose for which it was created. Thus there is a point of view from which it may be said that the glory of a table is that it shall be an outstandingly good table, or a ship that it shall weather wind and tide. Similarly, the greatest glory which can come to men is that we shall become like God, for to this end were we created.

In view of the foregoing our task is not to proudly assert our independence, but to find freedom through life in harmony with the Infinite. Man's freedom is *for* God and *in* God, not *against* God. We depend on him both because we must, and because we love to. We seek to do his will as good children seek to do the will of their parents, "for God hath not given us the spirit of fear; but of power and of love, and of a sound mind," and "hath saved us, and called us with a holy calling, not according to our works, but according to his own purpose and grace, which was given us in Christ Jesus before the world began."[6]

27

In the humility born of reflections such as these worship is spontaneous, and when worship is at its best we lose all sense of pride or of the oppression of fate. We feel ourselves eager to get in tune with the movement of life and with the love that throbs at the heart of the universe. Our common human life takes on a new significance, the various aspects of life assume their proper proportion, tensions relax, and we find ourselves possessed by a blessed peace. Yet it is not the stagnant kind of relaxation; rather it is energy without friction. We find ourselves doing our best without having to fight with ourselves.

This is so because only in worship do we truly find ourselves. "O Lord, . . . Thou madest us for Thyself, and our heart is restless, until it repose in Thee."[7] We do not know what becomes us until we know we are the children of our Father. Man is by virtue of the fact that God is for him and with him. Until a man knows and worships God he is imperfect and incomplete.

By way of contrast to this picture of a God of personal relationship we might note a statement by a modern Jewish rabbi. In an article entitled "Have We Outgrown God?" Rabbi Roland B. Gittelsohn says that modern man must throw away ideas that God is a person or a supernatural being.[8] He suggested we should think of God as a force or energy instead of a personal being. But how can anyone worship an impersonal force like electricity or atomic energy? We use the energy of electricity every time we turn on the electric light, but there is nothing there to which we would go to seek vision, forgiveness, renewal. It is in worship to a God who hears and answers prayer and can come unto us that the highest and most significant truths about life are made known.

Let us consider what happens when the heart of our own purpose is to discover and relate ourselves to the purposes of such a God. Then we believe that no greater goal in life than this can be carried forward to our children and our companions; we seek to awaken in them a passion for God and for godly things. We put them in the way of communion with Divinity. We teach them to look beyond us to him, and beyond the social order to his kingdom. Although their vision is likely to be limited because of their contact with us, the way of their lives is likely to be progressive because of their contact with him. Because the major purpose of our lives is to discover and accept the purpose of God for us, our first and most important aim is to incline the hearts of our children toward God, through worship, that they may learn of him and learn to live for the sake of things dear to him.

Beautiful as this world is, it has not yet achieved its full beauty. Can it be that, like us, the universe is still in process of creation, and that its full maturity awaits the time when we can cooperate fully with God in making the world even better than it was when it came from his hands? We seem to have a hint of this in the work of Burbank, who joined with God to produce new manifestations of plant life. In the same way our engineers are changing the course of rivers and the face of the earth, our chemists are bringing new colors to life, our inventors are giving new meanings to time and distance, and our physicists are releasing the latent power of the sun. Thoughts such as these lead to one conclusion of which we are convinced, that in spite of the mismanagement of men this is the best of all possible worlds — in the sense that it is the kind of world in which we can learn to be like God. It is not complete and final. It is the result of the operation of certain laws backed by creative purpose, and if we can learn these laws, we can share in its creation. It is in such a world as this that we can grow to be like God, both in the sense of desiring goodness and truth and also in the sense of bringing new relationships and new beauties into being.[9]

1. Leo Tolstoy, *Anna Karenina* (London House, 1939), p. 936.
2. I John 4:8.
3. Col. 1:16.
4. I Cor. 2:9.
5. D. and C. 76:5 e.
6. II Tim. 1:7, 9.
7. *The Confessions of Saint Augustine*, Edward B. Pusey, Jr. (New York: Pocket Books, 1957) Book I, page 1.
8. *Saturday Review*, September 16, 1961, p. 21.
9. For more complete discussion of this point see *Fundamentals*, by the author, pp. 11-25; also John 1:3; I Nephi 1:8; and D. and C. 85:2, 90:1, 75:5 a, b.

4 The Purpose of Life Revealed in Jesus Christ

A BOUT TWO THOUSAND years ago Jesus of Nazareth went about his native land of Palestine doing good,[1] bearing the sickness of men and healing their infirmities. He was a true man in all that goes to make up human nature. Yet those nearest to him gradually discovered by the authority of his word and works, by the miracles of his love and judgment, and most of all by his victory over death, that he was also the eternal Son of God. These first disciples came to believe that Jesus was more than man through their experience with him while he yet walked with them. Later, when he had risen from the dead, they looked back and realized that his resurrection was but the flowering of the life which he had lived in their presence. Their conviction of his divinity has been passed on to us, and every year has made their insight more credible.

JESUS IS THE KEY TO UNDERSTANDING

Sooner or later all Christian thinking about life brings us back to Jesus Christ. The Hebrew letter calls him "the author and finisher of our faith,"[2] but he is more than that. He is the key to all our understanding. He is the essential clue to the meaning of life.

Jesus is completely unique. He is quite unexplained either by his earthly ancestry or by his environment. He is

31

the Son of God who became like us that we might be like him. This truth about Jesus is decisively set forth in the scriptures:

> Let this mind be in you, which was also in Christ Jesus; who being in the form of God, thought it not robbery to be equal with God; but made himself of no reputation, and took upon him the form of a servant, and was made in the likeness of men; and being found in fashion as a man, he humbled himself, and became obedient unto death, even the death of the cross. Wherefore God also hath highly exalted him, and given him a name which is above every name; that at the name of Jesus every knee should bow, of things in heaven, and things in earth, and things under the earth; and that every tongue should confess that Jesus Christ is Lord, to the glory of God the Father.[3]
>
> God, who at sundry times and in divers manners spake in time past unto the fathers by the prophets, hath in these last days spoken unto us by his Son, whom he hath appointed heir of all things, by whom also he made the worlds; who being the brightness of his glory, and the express image of his person, and upholding all things by the word of his power, when he had by himself purged our sins, sat down on the right hand of the Majesty on high; being made so much better than the angels, as he hath by inheritance obtained a more excellent name than they:[4]

Jesus is the supreme revelation of Divinity, our clearest and best picture of what God is like. We get a faint glimpse of the nature of Divinity as we study a crystal through a microscope and see its order, beauty, and symmetry. More of God is revealed to us in the flowers and the trees where the grace of life is wedded to the truth of life. A yet higher revelation awaits us in the lives of the animals where there are rudimentary evidences of intelligence and of affection. Infinitely more of God is revealed to us in men, and particularly in good men, where the sense of right dawns clear, where conscience speaks, where love becomes a spiritual flame, where choice leads to nobility and the true glory of the soul begins to shine forth. More and more we see what God is like as we mount up the scale of being, but the revelation is still incomplete until we see Jesus. To see him truly is to see God manifest in all the splendor of his glory.[5]

OUR GREAT EXAMPLE

It is of vital importance to our spiritual life that we shall think of Jesus, after the manner of Paul, as the supreme revelation of the Father. But in our present field of concern we need to think of him, also, as the supreme revelation of true manhood. All other men have been tainted by sin. Paul himself says that "all have sinned, and come short of the glory of God."[6] Because of this, no mere man can be our example in any final sense. Only the Lord Jesus can show us what it means to fulfill the purpose of God in our creation. But he does this gladly. He says, "I call you not servants [those who toil blindly at the bidding of someone else, and for a purpose which they do not understand] but . . . friends [sharing the purpose of his life]; for all things that I have heard of my Father I have made known unto you."[7]

When I was a boy the physical education instructor at high school once told me to stand up straight. I did my best, but still he was not satisfied. Finally, he pulled my shoulders back until I stood as I should. Then he said, "Now, Edwards, get the 'feel' of that. Be sure you remember it. Next time I tell you to straighten up, keep on straightening until you feel as you do now." Our heavenly Father has done something like this for us. His guidance for us is not confined to words of instruction coming through the prophets and apostles. It is illustrated in the life of his Son, who is the living picture of what is meant by the command of God that we shall live rightly. Moreover, he has filled us with his Spirit and has given us the "feel" of sonship. When we live at our best, then by his grace we achieve within ourselves a sense of what it means truly to belong to him. We will

33

slump back into our old habits from time to time, but these times will become fewer, and one day we shall stand straight.

> Behold, what manner of love the Father hath bestowed upon us that we should be called the sons of God; therefore the world knoweth us not, because it knew him not. Beloved, now are we the sons of God, and it doth not yet appear what we shall be; but we know that, when he shall appear, we shall be like him; for we shall see him as he is.[8]

OUR PURPOSE IS TO BE LIKE GOD

The purpose of God revealed in the life and ministry of the Lord Jesus Christ is that we shall be like him. No achievement elsewhere can ever be an adequate substitute for this. No long prayers, not even moral goodness of itself is sufficient to meet the demands of our highest possibilities. The rich young man who kept the moral law from his youth still could not be perfect until he let this life of unblemished purity burst into passionate discipleship. The change needed to achieve this is so great that no other phrase expresses it quite so well as the one Jesus used, to be "born again." This is what Paul meant when he wrote, "I live; yet not I, but Christ liveth in me; and the life which I now live in the flesh I live by the faith of the Son of God, who loved me, and gave himself for me."[9]

The Christian faith is squarely opposed to any notion that men are able to redeem themselves. At various times such a suggestion has been put forth; but always it has been rejected by the conscience and experience of the church. When Christianity was yet young there arose a heresy bearing the name of Pelagius, whose teachings could be summed up in the watchword: "Every man his own Savior; it is good to know of Christ, but he is by no means indispensable." The only trouble with this is that it is not true. Christ is indispensable. Without him we can do nothing. We are "dead in trespasses and sins"[10] and only he can quicken us to "newness of life."

34

We are the climax and goal of creation. All other things were made with our life and growth in mind. We have been given dominion over the lesser creations, and have been set to subdue and replenish the earth. Moreover, of mankind, as of no other part of creation, is it said that God watches over us, rejoices in our repentance, and places more worth upon our souls than upon all the world. Indeed, as Christian people we believe that our humanity has been forever dignified by the stupendous fact of the incarnation of the Son of God in flesh like our own. He who was in the beginning with God, and who was God, took on himself the limitations of flesh and blood that he might show us the reality of our kinship with Divinity and the boundless possibilities of righteousness and of excellence which lie before us.

---

1. Acts 10:38.
2. Heb. 12:2.
3. Phil. 2:5-11.
4. Heb. 1:1-4.
5. John 14:9.
6. Rom. 3:23.
7. John 15:15.
8. I John 3:1, 2.
9. Gal. 2:20.
10. Eph. 2:1.

5 | Our Purpose and the Holy Spirit

Much is said in both the Old and New Testaments about the Spirit of God, or the Holy Spirit, which is the power of God working in the world to carry out his purposes. The Spirit of God has been such an important factor in the lives of men and nations who have served God most faithfully that we cannot seriously consider the purpose of God in us unless we also consider the place which the Holy Spirit has in revealing and achieving this divine purpose.

The presence and power of God in our personal lives is felt and experienced through the Holy Spirit. One of the major purposes of the Old Testament record is to tell the story of the guidance of the Spirit of God in the history of the Hebrew people. The secret of their spiritual genius lies in the fact that they believed that God was seeking to guide them and that they were his children and therefore ought to respond to his guidance. We may be assured that God has not left himself without witness at any time among any people; and it is a pity that we cannot see all history from this viewpoint. Because we have lost the larger vision we frequently fail to perceive the kindly endeavors of God to determine the course of our lives, but

> "There is a divinity that shapes our ends,
> Rough-hew them how we will."[1]

Usually the hand of God is unobtrusive, but the observing man cannot fail to note it. Surely something other than luck explains the many trivial occurrences which have changed the story of mankind. We are told that the cackling of geese once saved Rome. The reason the common thistle has its place upon the Scottish coat of arms is attributed to the fact that an invading soldier cried out when pricked by a thistle, warned the Scottish garrison, and so saved the nation. The defeat of the Spanish Armada by Drake's insignificant fleet is commemorated and explained by a monument which bears the inscription, "God blew with his wind, and they were scattered." Napoleon was halted at Waterloo by the genius and fortitude of Wellington and Blucher, but their devotion was made effective because it rained that day.

It is astounding to watch how the gifts of outstanding men — and sometimes even ungodly men — have promoted the advance of the race. The great railroad magnates, the empire builders of a generation ago, were not godly men. In sheer plundering selfishness they pushed forward in the forefront of the tide of empire. But in spite of their selfishness the railroads which they built united east and west and contributed toward the development of a great nation. Can this be entirely accidental? Are we not led to believe that behind the selfishness and blindness of these men was an overruling providence?

Beyond question the gifts of great men have been used to bring their fellows together and to promote greater brotherhood and understanding. But the talents of these men have not been created by themselves. They have been the gifts of God. The genius for organization, the vision which sees distant points united when their union seems impossible, the power to command men, the naked courage which attempts the impossible — these and all similar gifts come from without. No one on earth knows the final reason why one man is more able than another. We may point out how certain ones have obeyed the conditions of success while others have failed by refusing to obey. We may emphasize the importance of preparing for such endowment as Divinity cares to give. But we must nevertheless face the fact that God — for his own purposes — endows such as he sees fit to endow. The spirit "bloweth where it listeth."

PROGRESS IN HISTORY

As we look carefully at the testimony of history from the vantage point of the disciple, we can see an unceasing purpose running through the ages, and history therefore becomes especially worth studying. It has a plot. It leads somewhere. In spite of discouragements and frequent reversals, progress is real. History reveals how God has chosen to educate and discipline us. We have been free to act, and we have done so, and our rebellion has been followed by disaster after disaster. But God also has been free to act. He has surrounded us with inducements to righteousness. He has whispered his wishes, and some men have listened. Progress has not been an accidental thing, but a movement guided by God. "Holy men of God spake as they were moved by the Holy Ghost,"[2] and these prophets and seers have been far more significant figures in the march of men toward the heights than the generals or even the statesmen.

Very rarely have we or our fellows been given any detailed view of the future. Preknowledge is not nearly so necessary as we sometimes think, for while we do not know all, we know enough to go ahead. A traveler in Switzerland tells us that, uncertain of his way, he asked a small boy by the roadside where Kandersteg lay. "I do not know where Kandersteg is," said the boy, "but there is the road to it." That is an epitome of the spiritual experience of man. The goal has not yet been exactly located, but we know that it lies ahead and that the Spirit of God is ever ready to guide us on the way.

While it is sometimes hard to believe, a discriminating survey of history convinces us that this universe of ours is essentially an arena of spiritual conflict in which we are gradually achieving a higher order of life. Here we are not merely preparing for some other life, but for life now which is part of the life which is beyond. Here we are not called to achieve some mystic quality called spirituality, but to be spiritual. We are here to work out the divine purpose through the means which are at hand and in association with each other. Our most real progress has not been in wealth, resources, military force, scientific technology, or national power. These are relatively superficial and frequently temporary. They must be made to minister to a more permanent human progress which is found in the right of the common man to live his life, to make his own home, to do his own work, to support his own family, and to grow in Christian character as he discharges this task in the spirit of Christ.

The Work of the Holy Spirit

It is the testimony of the scriptures as well as in harmony with our experience that God has striven with men by his Spirit from the beginning. But it is also our experience that

> God, who at sundry times and in divers manners spake in time past unto the fathers by the prophets, hath in these last days spoken unto us by his Son.[3]

Jesus is our supreme example and commander. While a function of the Spirit of God is to lead us into all truth,[4] the primary purpose of the Holy Spirit is to be to us all that the Lord Jesus was to his disciples when he was with them as a bodily presence. The Holy Spirit is the expression of the intimate and personal principle at the heart of Christianity. All are promised that we shall know the Christ by the power of the Comforter.[5] The Spirit visits us as Christ once did, urging us to live better lives, rebuking our sins, showing the beauty of holiness, bringing health, encouragement, and strength, and giving our lives cohesion and power as we yield ourselves completely to God's great purpose for us. The Spirit does not come for its own sake, but that we might see Christ.

In the days when Jesus was on earth many men refused his ministry and turned away from him. So also may we refuse the ministry of the Holy Spirit and deny its place in our lives. When we do this we are denying God and at the same time denying our best selves. We are turning from Christ, whose life is our best illustration of a normal man fulfilling the purpose of his being. On the other hand, if we yield to the guidance of the Spirit we enter progressively into our true heritage.

Christ is still in the world as a spiritual presence and still inspires men with high and noble purposes. He still prompts those who love him to undertake special tasks for him and so to dedicate and develop the gifts which he has given. He still inspires the devout thinker, the loyal worker, and the true artist. He is still the guide of preachers, of poets, and of common men. He still directs the work of his church in its great task of saving the world.

Toward Truth, Beauty, and Goodness

In our endeavor to see our own life purpose more clearly it is therefore extremely wise for us to look back over the stream of history under the guidance of the Spirit, and with the example of our Master ever before us, to cultivate the presence of Christ. As we do so we find that the Spirit has led many men from all walks of life into the pursuit of truth and beauty and goodness. Then as the Spirit turns our thoughts within we recognize that here we are confronted with this further expression of the purpose of life, that we too should be engaged in the pursuit of truth, beauty, and goodness.

40

When we consider the record made by the lovers of truth in every generation, our courage is renewed and our spirits rise in happy realization of the greatness achieved by some of our fellows. Who can help but be inspired by men such as the great and gentle John Huss, who defied the Pope, spoke out against corruption, and was burned at the stake declaring, "In the end truth will conquer." Truth has her list of martyrs in every age. Jeremiah, Paul, Livingston, Lincoln, Joseph Smith — these are the type of men found in that glorious company. For truth's sake both men of science and men of religion have always been found ready to make the supreme sacrifice. The brilliant thinking and courageous proclamation of these lovers of truth have led the way step by step out of darkness into light. Today we pay honor to such men and women. But the truth about things — facts — can never bring us to eternal life. Only the truth about God and man can do this. This is the truth which is the primary concern of the Holy Spirit.

Our heavenly Father has also spoken to us through the creations of the lovers of beauty, who have brought to us an understanding of his character and of his purpose in the world. It is difficult to define beauty; it is an emotional experience, an evidence of the ability of soul to speak to soul. Words are often inadequate, but music and painting and sculpture and poetry and architecture may provoke in those who have eyes to see and ears to hear "thoughts that do often lie too deep for tears." These things have not been made available to us without great sacrifice, but the faithfulness which beauty has inspired tells its own tale of high and noble courage. It is said that Mozart spent the last ten years of his life in the great pleasure-loving city of Vienna in extreme poverty. Sometimes he had no food, or even coal in winter. One cold morning he and his wife were found waltzing to keep warm. Yet when his publisher said to him: "Write in a more easy, popular style or I will not print a note or give you a cent," Mozart replied, "Then, sir, I have

41

only to resign myself and die of hunger." But not even Mozart can show us the winning beauty of eternal life. Only the Spirit of God can do this.

The lovers of truth and the lovers of beauty put our pettiness to shame, and the lovers of goodness stand in constant rebuke of our selfishness. These are they who feel the inner urge to righteousness and who give their lives willingly for the service of God and their fellows. Such men as Wilberforce, the hero of the opposition to slavery, and John Hampden, the hero of the battle against intolerable prison conditions, stand as representatives of one section of this great troop of men and women. But leading these and inspiring them are the prophets and seers who have sought and found God. Look through the "hall of fame" pictured in Chapter 11 of the letter to the Hebrews. Then carry on the story from the great sufferings of Paul to the last of the martyrs. Find place in your list for St. Francis and for Luther and John Bunyan and John Wesley and a host of others whose names few may know. All these were Spirit-guided lovers of goodness in action.

Transforming Power of the Spirit

To believe in the Holy Spirit is to believe that God is still at work in the world, and that he is inspiring and aiding us in the task of facing life as becomes the sons of God. The Spirit lays emphasis on the finer personal values. Under the guidance of this Spirit we not only see visions and dream dreams, but we also find new power for friendship, forbearance, charity, humility, and the other Christian graces. Under the guidance of this Spirit the purpose of life gradually becomes clear to us.

No material possessions nor any of the secondary manifestations of life itself explain the purpose of our creation. We do not live to make money. We do not live just to enjoy physical health. We are not created to be beautiful or that

42

we might shine among our fellows by reason of our social graces. All of these things are important in their proper places, but the purpose of life lies beyond them in ourselves and in our fellows. It lies in personality which is richer and finer than any we have yet known, personality cultivated in kindly and constructive relations with our fellows and in humble and worshipful relations with God. In the higher sense we are entering into life. We are beginning to be. Not in any external reward but in ourselves will lie the satisfaction of our strivings. The greatest reward of a good man is to be a good man, to feel within himself that to this end was he born.

1. Shakespeare, *Hamlet,* Act V.
2. II Peter 1:21.
3. Heb. 1:1, 2.
4. John 14:16, 17; 15:26.
5. I Cor. 12:3; John 15:26.

6 | The Church and the Purpose of Life

WHEN WE WERE yet children we were amused by the story of *Alice in Wonderland,* and many of us still remember the references to the Cheshire cat whose smile appeared first and then remained after the rest of him disappeared. The idea of a smile apart from a face, fantastic though it is, is no more fantastic than the idea of a person apart from a social group. All the finer aspects of personality — the things which we cherish most in the people whom we love and admire — are social qualities. Justice, mercy, brotherly kindness, and similar qualities are developed and find their significance in social relationships. We are born into a society where we are mutually dependent, we grow in the process of exchange, and we achieve greatness when we accept happily the obligations and privileges of our joint life.

SOCIAL LIFE BUILDS CHARACTER

Some years ago a noted educator, Dr. Blackmar of the University of Kansas, gave an address at the Stone Church in Independence on justifiable individualism. He asserted that the only justifiable individualism is that which is rooted deep in the social life of the time. Our experience confirms the validity of this insight. The individual and the group should not be in conflict with each other, but should be mutually helpful. The best good of the individual is as closely related to that of the group as breathing in is related to breathing out.

Personality is the process of coming out of one's self and living in others. Indeed, a man is truly himself only insofar as he has interests and investments in other people. Ingrown affection, self-centered interests, and unshared knowledge do not promote personality; they destroy it. But, on the other hand, all of the peculiarly human gifts have this one thing in common — they enable men to share each other's lives. They all tend to make for unity. Our literature, our music, our art, our science, and our inventions can all be abused; but in the lives of men of goodwill they serve to break down the barriers that divide and to unite us for the common good. The purpose of life is achieved only as we recognize that this mutual belonging, this inescapable togetherness, is a foreordained and beneficent thing. It is in the exchanges of our common life that the eternal qualities of character are shaped and matured.

That which is true socially is also true religiously. Spiritual life is based on spiritual fellowship. The New Testament shows no interest whatever in unattached Christians. The New Testament Christians took it for granted that "disciples" are brothers. Just as you cannot say "citizen" without implying the state, so you cannot say "Christian" without implying the church.

Blessed through Others

It is conceivable that our heavenly Father might cause us to live and grow under direct instruction from him. Indeed there are occasions when we are singularly blessed with the presence of his Holy Spirit. But this is by no means the only method used by him. *He prefers to bless us through our fellows,* and it is part of his plan to bless us as we join him in blessing others. This is clearly illustrated in the life of the church. Men do not believe in the gospel unless some-

45

one takes it to them. Behind every missionary is the church, and working through both the church and the individual is the Holy Spirit.

Our dependence on the church does not cease when we have been won to Christ. We are as dependent on the sustenance provided by the church as a newborn baby is dependent on the provision made by its family. Indeed, the concept of rebirth is basic to understanding why the ordinance of baptism by immersion has been so fittingly chosen both as the symbol and means of the new life in Christ. Those who have entered into the church continue their growth only by being "immersed" — deeply involved with others who have made similar commitments and who share the life purposes of the reborn.

The more we know of Jesus the more readily we can understand his purposes in building his church. The church was formed to continue his work in the world under the direction of the Holy Spirit. It is a divine creation rather than a human institution, and in this fact lies the hope of its effectiveness. The church bears the name of her Lord, transmits his life, teaches his laws, interprets his purposes, seeks his children, acts with his authority, and is the promise and precursor of his kingdom.

Since it is the nature of the man of God to find fullness of life with his fellows, the processes of salvation are inseparably connected with the church. When we are saved from the kingdom of sin and self-centeredness we must find our place in the kingdom of God, or we are a people without a spiritual country. When we are saved from the isolation, the insecurity, and the illusiveness of selfish purpose, it is the purpose of the Lord to recenter us in the best spiritual society. He does this by bringing us into his presence in the church which has been redeemed by him.

As we have already noted, it is the purpose of our heavenly Father to bless his children through helping us to minister to each other. What we do not so readily discern is that this concern that we shall be mutually helpful reaches across the generations and down the dispensations. This was a major emphasis in the early days of the Restoration. Because of this wise provision of our heavenly Father, many who are seemingly dead yet speak to us, and the communion of Saints — the fellowship which reaches across the ages — is a very real thing. This is enshrined in the heritage and traditions and life of the church.

The church reaches across the generations both to enrich our spiritual lives and to clarify our sense of the divine purpose in us. The scriptures have been safeguarded in this fashion. In addition, great hymns, religious art, the history which records the offerings made by many diverse Christians, the religiously-inspired activities which belong to generations rather than to any particular period (hospitals, schools, homes, and others) all owe their existence to organized religion and — among us — to the organized life of the Church of Jesus Christ.

No solitary man, and no single generation, can truly discern the purpose of God in the lives of men. In order to approach this as nearly as we may, we need to remember that there are fashions of thought and of speech in religion as in other matters which affect men in their personal and group life, and we need to seek the guidance of the "traditions of the elders" so that our tendency to be "tossed about with every wind of doctrine" shall be offset by the testimony of the ages. Only so shall we be safeguarded against the infiltration of shallow ideas about God and his purpose.

PERSONAL TASKS REMAIN

The church preaches the gospel, teaches its requirements, and heals many of our diverse sicknesses. It provides an

47

atmosphere in which worship is natural and where the forms of worship are available but not obtrusive. The church holds us up to the requirements of eternal life — reminding us, chiding us, judging us, helping us. But the church was not formed to be the repository and dispenser of a guaranteed salvation. Her purpose is to be the living and cooperative agent of redemption, while tasks and opportunities of personal righteousness remain with us as individuals.

One of the benefits which society confers on us is that it makes specialization possible. Robinson Crusoe on his desert island had no time to specialize. He had to be a jack-of-all-trades. Modern society on the other hand is built on specialization. The church likewise is built on a modified specialization. Each member lives and is sustained by the lifeblood which flows through the body. The richness of this life is made possible by the contribution of countless other members. But he and they each contribute according to their specialized gifts. "All are called according to the gifts of God unto them."[1] Paul has expressed this very beautifully in his letter to the Ephesians:

> He gave some, apostles; and some, prophets; and some, evangelists; and some, pastors and teachers; for the perfecting of the saints, for the work of the ministry, for the edifying of the body of Christ; till we, in the unity of the faith, all come to the knowledge of the Son of God, unto a perfect man, unto the measure of the stature of the fullness of Christ; that we henceforth be no more children, tossed to and fro, and carried about with every wind of doctrine, by the sleight of men, and cunning craftiness, whereby they lie in wait to deceive; but speaking the truth in love, may grow up into him in all things, which is the head, even Christ; from whom the whole body fitly joined together and compacted by that which every joint supplieth, according to the effectual working in the measure of every part, maketh increase of the body unto the edifying of itself in love.[2]

THE CHURCH AND THE PURPOSE OF LIFE

The church is an essential instrument in promoting the

divine purpose. It was divinely established and is divinely maintained. Its members are born of the spirit of light and truth and joined together in that same spirit. It draws on resources accumulated at great cost by many generations of devoted believers. It bears unceasing testimony that Jesus Christ is the Son of God and Savior of mankind, and provides great and diversified ministries which seek to express the mind and will of the Master. The church builds strength and fortitude in times of difficulty, and patience and restraint in times of crisis. It challenges the believers to service, requiring that each of us shall find his place and work there humbly, without undue concern regarding his own prominence but with deep concern regarding the task committed to him and to his fellows.

The church is different from any and all other institutions in that it ministers to deeper and more enduring needs than they. In our search for the meaning of the purpose of life we shall be wise if we conduct our personal search in the company of those who are similarly concerned to make life truly meaningful. United in the fellowship of the Spirit and enriched with the experience of the years, we shall discover the purposes of God in us as we could not possibly do on a solitary quest.

---

1. D. and C. 119:8 b.
2. Eph. 4:11-16.

7 | The Spirit and the Body

WORKING IN HIS garden one day, Francis of Assisi was asked what he would do if he was suddenly told that he was to die at sunset. Without hesitation Francis replied, "I would finish hoeing my garden." We need to emulate the wise and good Franciscan at this point. We are living here and now. This is our day of opportunity and of testing, and our eternal purpose must be constantly interpreted in terms of the present situation. Once we face the fact that we are here for a purpose and relate that purpose to our daily life, each and all of our several activities fit into a nobler and more meaningful pattern.

Two Temptations

Christians have always faced two related temptations. The first of these is the temptation to regard the needs of the body too highly. This expresses itself in the tendency to satisfy our physical appetites, to seek pleasures as ends in themselves, and to pursue ease and comfort at too great a cost. Many Christians have interpreted the gospel as a means to prosperity and security, bringing peace of mind, positive personal power, and successful adjustment to the conflicting demands of our times. This is no modern point of view. This same attitude has given rise down the ages to the presumption that social service and the healing of the body are

50

ultimate evidences of Christianity. "By their fruits ye shall know them," has been interpreted many times as meaning that the truth of the gospel is shown in the physical and material evidences of the blessing of God — and this despite the fact that the Son of God had nowhere to lay his head.[1]

The second temptation is to regard the body as of no importance whatever or even as the root cause of sin. This expresses itself in asceticism, monasticism, and otherworldliness. The earliest heresies of the Christian church denied the reality of the physical life of Jesus because it was too earthly. The Docetists claimed that Jesus only *appeared* to be human. Even Paul struggled with the relationship of man in the "flesh" and in the spirit.

Both of these attitudes can be carried to the extreme. There is no serious question that the whole material order was created for a good purpose.[2] In view of the weight of evidence throughout the scriptures, we must recognize the rightful significance of the body. But we must not give it either too much or too little importance in the total scheme of things. The whole person has its place in the purposes of God. When the Son of God took upon himself the human body, he forever bore witness to the sacramental nature of our bodily life. One of the striking lessons of the resurrection is that material things have a permanent spiritual value and significance, and that there can be no true redemption in man's life unless his material existence is also redeemed.

SPIRITUAL AND PHYSICAL INTERDEPENDENCE

When we look forward to the fulfillment of the great promises of the scriptures we realize that the return of our Master to this earth will be personal and visible. The disciples who watched the ascension were told: "This same Jesus, which is taken up from you into heaven, shall so come in like manner as ye have seen him go into heaven."[3] This is readily believable when we remember that the return of Christ is part of the great movement in which he will "make all things new,"[4] and in which he will be hailed as their Redeemer by those who have long waited for the redemption of their bodies.[5] It is for this reason that modern revelation emphasizes the fact that "the spirit and the body is the soul of man."[6] Further, through latter-day prophecy it is affirmed that "the elements are eternal, and spirit and element, inseparably connected, receiveth a fullness of joy; and when separated, man can not receive a fullness of joy."[7]

God breathed into man the breath of life, and he became a living soul.[8] The choices that we make are registered in nerve and sinew, and become habits from which we can hardly escape. Our highest aspirations and our noblest purposes are directly influenced by our physical resources. It is for this reason that our heavenly Father has advised us regarding what we shall eat, about the avoidance of habit-forming drugs, and about the importance of health and rest.[9] The wealth of instruction which we have received in connection with the avoidance of intemperate passion has great significance at this point.

The "body" includes our skills and aptitudes as well as our physical frames. These are extremely important in the divine scheme of things as well as in the human. It is not enough, for example, that we shall have compassion on our less fortunate fellows. We must make our compassion effective. This means, for example, that the doctor must be trained in observation and in skill. He must be able to determine the true nature of an illness and apply the remedy, whether it be rest, medicine, or surgery. Without such skills his compassion is empty emotion.

One of the most insistent needs of today is the need for a sense of craftsmanship — of delight in good workmanship. The craze for mass production and the tragedy of overspecialization have combined to rob most of us of any abiding joy in the products of our skill. Work has become drudgery, and a

52

large section of life has lost its creative possibilities. Our just pride in artistic endeavor has been stolen by the machine, and many have never learned to use their leisure so as to find the pride in the worthy achievement which our fathers knew.

The Bell Laboratories have developed a machine which seems to represent all too faithfully much of our life today. On the desk of one of the executives is a small wooden box with a single switch on one side. When the switch is pushed there is a buzzing sound, and the lid slowly rises so that a hand can emerge. The hand then reaches down and turns off the switch and the buzzing ceases while the hand slips quietly back into the box. That is all there is to it. The contraption merely makes a noise and then shuts itself off. Yet it reminds us — which is its purpose — of the day-to-day existence of so many in our world for whom activity and noise have become an end in themselves.

The mutual dependence of spirit and body works both ways. Discipline of the body for the sake of improving its competence has an immediate effect on the spirit. On the other hand, every spiritual advance should be registered in material adjustment. No such advance is secure until it is registered in patterns of living and in social institutions. The surge of missionary passion should be marked by testimony and the payment of tithing. The joy of the promised kingdom should lead to the acquisition of definite and practical skills for the kingdom's sake.

TRUTH EMBODIED IN ACTION

To be "living souls" engaged in creative tasks is to constantly acquire new vision and to match this new vision with new power to make the vision come true. This is what lies behind the Bible and Book of Mormon doctrine that our earthly life is a time of probation. We are here to face the facts of life, to build, not just to dream. We are hear to learn the

53

disciplines of achievement, to share the fellowship of conquest, and to grow in our learning and in our sharing.

With our heavenly Father, love is not just an emotion but it is a way of acting. Among us, similarly, spirituality must be more than a feeling of elation such as we enjoy in prayer meeting. It must be a full way of living in which spiritual purpose is manifest in godly action. Life will not let us jump to conclusions. The truth as it is in the Lord Jesus is only fully understood when it also becomes a way of behavior. Indeed, we only learn the truth as we learn to apply it to the problems which beset us. Not until the truth is embodied in life, and illuminated thereby, is it really ours.

Without doubt much of the insight and many of the tools which are necessary to human progress have already been developed. Yet our experience has been that our progress in the physical and scientific realms has often led toward catastrophe, so that each sentence in the story of progress has been punctuated by conflict. When we realize this, we recognize once more our absolute dependence upon God. The most significant factor in human life in any generation is the faith of that generation. We need such faith to monitor our advance. As it is, there is much great wealth which does not serve humanity; there is much of beauty which does not administer to character; there is much of truth which is not harnessed to human needs. So long as this remains true we shall be spiritually anemic as well as physically impoverished. Riches of any kind must serve humanity, and this only happens when they include riches of the spirit. The spirit and the body belong together, and the purpose of God is concerned with both.

This purpose now begins to stand clear. It is a spiritual purpose, but it is not merely a matter of dreams, nor yet of the promise of another world. The purpose of life is to live as God lives. Our heavenly Father has loving concern for all his creation and expresses this concern in sacrificial helpfulness. He not only loves men, but he makes his love count for their salvation. He not only wants to save us, but he knows how to save us. He not only knows how, but he does it — even if it means dying for us that we might live.

Our purpose in life is to respond to the call to sonship with all that we have and are. Man is not a body in which the spirit happens to dwell. He is not a spirit which happens to have been trapped in a body. Body and spirit are both gifts of God. Each needs the other for a "fullness of joy."

---

1. Matt. 8:20.
2. Gen. 1:33; 2:2.
3. Acts 1:11.
4. Rev. 21:5.
5. Rom. 8:21, 23.
6. D. and C. 85:4 a.
7. D. and C. 90:5 e.
8. Gen. 2:8.
9. D. and C. 86; 42:12; 119:3, 9.

8 Higher Levels of Life

ONE CANNOT READ the New Testament without being impressed by the way in which the entire level and meaning of life is raised from the incidents of the body to the experiences of the Spirit. In the New Testament community Jesus ministered among living people, and yet said that he had come "that they might have life."[1] What then did he mean by "life"? In one of his most famous passages Paul wrote, "to be carnally minded is death; but to be spiritually minded is life and peace."[2] John, too, wrote, "We have passed from death unto life, because we love the brethren."[3] Evidently Jesus, Paul, and John were using the term "life" in a deeper sense than we usually do. According to them one may be in vigorous bodily health and yet be dead, having been killed by sin, not disease. Life in the fullest sense of the word involves living in response to the Spirit of God; living on higher levels than the instinctive or habitual.

The growth of our genius and the development of our resources has led to a vast enlargement of the pleasures of life. As an aid to further achievement, pleasure is excellent; as a competitor with the best, pleasure is a dangerous enemy. There is a constant pressure in modern society to cease our striving and enjoy the comforts of greater leisure and prosperity. All this is to be desired so long as delight in these pleasures does not cause us to seek them at the expense of life itself.

We are indebted to the Danish theologian and philosopher Kierkegaard for a parable which brings into sharp relief how we can forget our high calling and be content with lower things. Kierkegaard says that a wild duck was flying with his mates in the springtime, northward across Europe. On the flight he happened to come down in a barnyard in Denmark where there were tame ducks. He ate and enjoyed some of their corn, and stayed — first for an hour, and then for a day, and then for a week, and then for a month, and finally, because he liked the good fare and the safety of the barnyard, he stayed on through the summer. But one autumn day his wild mates were wending their way southward again and passed over the barnyard. He heard their cries, and this stirred him with a strange thrill of joy and desire. Flapping his wings, he rose in the air to join his old comrades in their flight to the land of summer. But, alas, he found that his good fare and easy living had made him so soft and heavy that he could rise no higher than the eaves of the barn. So he sank back into the barnyard, saying to himself, "Oh, well, my life is safe here and the fare is good." Every spring and again every autumn when the wild ducks flew over his barnyard and he heard their honking cry, his eyes gleamed for a moment and he began to lift his wings and would have joined his former friends if he could have. But at length the day came when the wild ducks flew over him and uttered their call and he paid not the slightest attention to them.

A Challenging Task

Much of our social reform has comfort and security as its keynote. We think of pensions, adequate hospitalization, and a shorter workweek. All these things are good, if — but the "if" is very significant. These things are good if we develop with them challenges which will stimulate us in the days of our maturity. Children should be protected and educated. Older people who have fought the battle of life should be safeguarded in the enjoyment of its rewards. But the primary need of mature men and women in the full flower of their strength is challenge. We want time for necessary leisure, but no time just to waste. We want a chance to work near to our capacity, not always in the mental realm but at least on an exalted plane which calls for clear thinking, deep feeling, and effective craftsmanship. We need to hear and to respond to the call for new worlds to conquer. We shall damn ourselves if we build a world in which heroism is no longer required and where the best of life is given over to middling virtues and prearranged satisfactions. One of God's greatest gifts to man is a world where there are challenging tasks to which one may respond with his best.

When we give ourselves time and opportunity for contemplation, and particularly when we are in the presence of God, we know in our hearts that the pursuit of pleasure or comfort alone cannot satisfy us. In youth we seek for greater physical powers, to be "grown up," to be strong or beautiful. Then as maturity advances we seek larger intellectual and social adjustments, the power to think and to plan and to reason. As the real meanings of life unfold, even these become secondary, and the purpose of life speaks to us in terms of self-control and self-dedication in harmony with a worthy task. We are not "grown up" in the spiritual sense until we seek the higher spiritual values even at the expense of present pain. Paul says: "Woe is unto me, if I preach not the gospel! . . . a dispensation of the gospel is committed unto me."[4] His ministry cost him scourgings and shipwrecks and prison and death itself, yet he knew that he would be untrue to the larger purpose of his creation if he was untrue to the task God had given him.

JOY

Quite frequently we use the terms "pleasure" and "joy" interchangeably. When we are speaking or writing carefully, however, we distinguish between the two words. Pleasure has primary reference to gratification of the senses or mind or to agreeable sensations or emotions. Pleasure always has a sensuous flavor. Joy, on the other hand, points toward an exultation of spirit—happiness, felicity, ecstasy. Neither pleasure nor joy should be goals of endeavor. They are by-products, not purpose. If we seek them for their own sake they elude us constantly as though frightened by our eagerness. But joy functions on a higher level than does pleasure.

The Book of Mormon tells us that "men are, that they might have joy."[5] Joy differs from happiness in terms of its depth of emotional fulfillment and its basic spiritual nature. Paul spoke of himself as sorrowful yet always rejoicing. It has been said of some few people that they are "so full of joy that they can afford to be serious." Joy is rooted deep in the emotional and spiritual life and can endure any temporary mood.

Jesus loved good health and spent a good deal of time healing people's bodies. He was happy in good reading and was at home in the best literature of his time. He enjoyed friendship and social life — we know that he was the guest of honor at the wedding of his friends. Yet while he did not despise these passing joys he was always willing to sacrifice them for the greater joys arising from the satisfaction of overcoming his moral enemies, an increase in his usefulness to others, the approval of persons of good quality, and most of all, for a sense of the approval of Divinity.

The most significant fact about the joy of our Master is that its sources were not at the mercy of men or circumstances. Poor, homeless, about to be crucified, Jesus could still say to his disciples, "These things have I spoken unto you, . . . that your joy might be full."[6] Joy such as this gives us a hint of the final purpose of life. It was a joy arising out of his trust in his Father, out of his boundless hope for the future, out of his sense of divine approval, and out of his happiness in watching men quicken into new life as they came to know God. The purpose of life includes the achievement of these sources of abiding joy.

PAIN AND SUFFERING

Whenever we consider the possibility of a radiantly joyful life, a truly happy life, we naturally think of Jesus; and yet his life led to a cross! We do not fully understand; but whatever may be said of pain and suffering, it is the route that Jesus chose. Pain discourages and turns back many whose faith is not sufficiently resolute or whose courage will not stand the test. Yet pain seems to be necessary to the development of our lives. Pain seems to be part of the warp and woof of life.

Arnold Toynbee offers a very sound explanation concerning the place of suffering in the lives of Christians by comparing the Christians' attitude with that of the Buddhists, especially those in the older, more conservative school. The basic belief of Buddhists is that suffering is the product of desire and can be completely abolished only by completely extinguishing desire as well. Their ultimate goal, what they consider the true end of man, is to eliminate suffering which means to extinguish desire of all kinds.

In contrast, Christianity distinguishes between self-centered desires, which are bad and ought to be destroyed, and self-sacrificing desires which are good and should be acted upon no matter what the cost in suffering. The highest goal for man as seen by Christianity is not to eliminate all desires and thus all suffering, but to follow the promptings of man's good desires — to be guided by love, even though it leads to a cross. For the true Christian to incur suffering is a lesser evil than to annihilate love. There are even times when the suffering of one who endures for the sake of love can become a positive good. This is recognized in the observation made many years ago, and many times repeated, that "the blood of the martyrs is the seed of the church." He who suffers for love lives in harmony with the God of love who gave his Son to suffer that therein the depth of the divine love might be fully revealed. By following the example of the Son of God, his disciple may help to arouse in other souls the rightful response of love.[7]

Epictetus, a cripple and the slave of a brutal master, nevertheless became one of the greatest of the stoic philosophers. None of his writings have survived, but his teachings emphasize a love of practical goodness in such fashion that he still has influence among men of goodwill. Yet he served his generation in spite of all sorts of difficulties. One of the same character was John Milton, who came under the severe discipline imposed by his blindness, but who yet wrote for all mankind, "They also serve who only stand and wait."[8] Some of the greatest spiritual advances have been won out of the heart of struggle and pain.

A HIGHER LOYALTY

Most of us are activity-oriented. We are set on achievement, on doing something. It is a most unusual person who plans his life to be merely a good average Christian. We dream great dreams of service and devotion, but disappointment and disillusionment always seem to come. Many of us come to recognize greater values in accomplishments we did not at first appreciate. Very few, however, achieve the heights we once dreamed, and many fail so completely that this failure is likely to bring a sense of futility. It is certain to do so if personal success and the honor of making a contribution have been our real goals. We are saved from being governed by success or failure only when we do not occupy the center of the picture ourselves. Our need is for a sense of proportion which helps us know what is worthwhile and so worthy of transcending loyalty.

When the ruined city of Pompeii was excavated the

61

archaeologists discovered a skeleton in full armor and clutching a spear and a shield with bony fingers, still standing at what had been the assigned post of the living soldier. No other human remains were found near that skeleton. All the other inhabitants of that brilliant resort — merchants, officials, nobles, priests — had fled for safety before the impending horror. The soldier alone stood fast in the path of the great disaster. Loyalty held him to his post while the whole world dissolved in fire. Is there not something here finer than life itself? Had not this man learned the meaning of loyalty so truly that even the centuries could not bury him? Today, and rightfully, he speaks to us of values which we must conserve no matter what pain they cost.

What Happens in Us

It may not be part of the divine purpose that each one of us shall win the approval of history on his outstanding work. But it is part of the divine purpose that we shall each become great in the quality of our inner selves. This requires that we shall not put "success" first. At the turn of the century Horatio Alger made the symbol and dream of America the poor boy who through hard work and honesty achieved great success and the hand of the boss's daughter. But the truth is that not everyone can succeed. Even though we may obey the conditions of success we cannot command it. Success is a matter first of ability and training and peculiar adaptation to the task. Hard work and good intentions are not necessarily enough. Next it is a matter of opportunity or of providence or of what some people call luck. Failure at any one of these points may easily mean failure all along the line. Lack of ability, lack of opportunity, or lack of adaptation may prevent our achievement. So may any one of a thousand things over which we have little or no control. But whatever happens to our achievement is of no primary importance. It is not what happens *to* us, but what happens *in* us that is important.

Our present earthly life is but a small segment of eternity. It is important primarily because the trends of life are determined here. God is not primarily concerned with our temporary material success. Nor should we be so completely concerned as we sometimes are. When we look at things from the vantage point of our heavenly Father we do not need to fear present failure as many of us do so desperately. What we need to fear is a failure of courage to continue. We must exert every effort to find the best, to do the best, and to be the best. All else is failure. If we do continue to strive then, though our works are burned, we shall be saved;[9] it is in us that God is interested. We must promote his glory. We must live lives turned toward him. Such living will be effective even though we are not permitted to make the specific offerings that we would like to make.

Let us remember that salvation is not freedom from sorrow, but freedom from sin. It is not the absence of pain, but the presence of spiritual power. It is not the free gift of God in the sense that it costs us nothing, but it is character achieved by the grace of God. The apostles realized this when, enduring torture, and fearful that they might yield to their pain, they prayed, "Grant unto thy servants, that with all boldness they may speak thy words."[10] The great and romantic figures of history have realized this in part, and have always preferred death to treason.

Pursuit of the highest values of life demands courage and resolute determination. It is the spirit which urged the great Ulysses "to strive, to seek, to find, and not to yield." But it is perhaps best expressed for most of us in the immortal words of the three Hebrew young men whom Nebuchadnezzar threatened to cast into the fiery furnace:

> Our God whom we serve is able to deliver us from the burning fiery furnace, and he will deliver us out of thine hand,

O king. But if not, be it known unto thee, O king, that we will not serve thy gods, nor worship the golden image which thou hast set up.[11]

The creation of persons of such caliber justifies all the travail of the years.

1. John 10:10.
2. Rom. 8:6.
3. I John 3:14.
4. I Cor. 9:16, 17.
5. II Nephi 1:115.
6. John 15:11.
7. Arnold Toynbee, *Christianity Among the Religions of the World* (New York: Charles Scribners Sons, 1957), pp. 24-25.
8. Milton, "On His Blindness."
9. I Cor. 3:15.
10. Acts 4:29.
11. Daniel 3:17, 18.

9 | Purpose and Immortality

THERE IS A PURPOSE in our creation. This purpose is an expression of the love of God, and is to the glory of God and to our salvation. This salvation reaches beyond life as we now know it. Indeed, it must do so or many of our finest efforts are subject to the caprice of death.

DEATH IS A FRIEND

There is an ancient legend that in the old sweet days before men knew death they lived in gladsome idleness; they played, they sang, they loved, they danced in a life that had no gravity and no greatness. But when death came, new meaning came into life. Time took on new value; affection, by growing more serious, became nobler; men thought of themselves more worthily and of their deeds more truly when they saw that a night would come when they could work no longer. Friends and families lived in a more tender light when the sun was known to shine but for a season; earth became lovelier when men realized that the places which knew them now would soon know them no more. The limit set to time drove their thought out toward eternity. The Voice of Death who was to claim them bade them live in earnest, made them feel that there was something greater than play. Death breathed into life the spirit out of which all

65

tragic and all heroic things have emerged. The horizon which limited life defined it and made it great.

Without debating the application of this story in detail we can agree that it does present one thing clearly — the important fact that while death must be reckoned with, it is a friend and not an enemy. Immortality is desirable only when we have learned to use life nobly.[1] Death rescues us from an earthly immortality for which we are not yet prepared, and so adds to the glory and the grandeur of life. If a soul made for eternity were to be withered by time, would not that be an even greater tragedy than the coming of death, which separates us from our loved ones for a time, but is powerless to keep us apart after they, too, have met Death's summons and have known the true meaning of his call?

Death is a friend, the messenger of immortality. This messenger will not always be needed; even now, we do not welcome him before his time. Indeed, we long for the day when his services will be no longer necessary. But in our present situation when we learn that death is just a messenger and not an executioner, we are saved from bondage brought about by fear.[2]

LIFE AND IMMORTALITY

If, as we believe, death calls us to a life beyond, it is evident that the purpose of God in our creation must be understood in the light of immortality. But is this great hope truly believable? Many of the greatest men of the ages have thought so — such men as Socrates, Plato, Cicero, Marcus Aurelius, Augustine, Aquinas, Luther, Isaac Newton, Tennyson, Wadsworth, Emerson, and a host of others. It was the last named of these who assured as that "what is excellent as God lives, is permanent"; on another occasion, Emerson wrote: "Our dissatisfaction with any other solution is the blazing evidence of immortality."

When Saint Augustine, the apostle of England, had fairly achieved the conversion of the Kingdom of Kent, he sent some of his fellow missionaries to attempt the conversion of the Kingdom of Northumbria. At first the king and his couriers were disinclined even to give the missionaries a hearing, but presently one counselor, wiser than the others, addressed the king as follows: "Thou knowest, O King, that ofttimes on a winter's night, when we are assembled in this dimly lighted hall a swallow will come from the night, pass swiftly from darkness into the light and out again into darkness. So it is with the human soul. We came we know not whence, we pass through this dimly lighted earthly existence, and then we go swiftly out again, we know not whither. If, therefore, these new teachers can tell us aught concerning whence we came or whither we go, it were well to hear them."[3]

BORN FOR ETERNITY

Our highest capacities and our highest experiences unite us with the world beyond the limits of time. We were born for eternity. We are akin to the eternal Spirit who is from everlasting to everlasting. Once we respond to the demands of our own better nature and live as though this were true, we find that the purpose of life is again enlarged. We are lifted above the immediacy of the present and are saved from the tyranny of petty things. Life takes on scope and dignity. We are no longer content to eat, drink, and be merry, and we begin to live with a view to all that is to come.

A good man is the finest product of life as we know it. It is irrational to think that death ends our personal existence. If it does, then we stand "half built against the skies," something great which has only been started, a prophecy which will never be fulfilled. We dream greater dreams, think greater thoughts, love with a deeper love than can ever be realized if death is the final end. Have we come this far only to be cheated of our finest and most persistent hope? Would the majesty of creation end in such a mockery? "Unless there is a way for the continuance of the human self, the world is full of the blunt edges of human meanings, the wreckage of human values, and therefore the failures of God."[3]

Christian experience and testimony form one great chorus of protest against the idea that a man dies with the death of his body. The man who loses an arm is terribly handicapped, but he does not feel that any part of his true self has been amputated. Helen Keller is limited in perception and expression by reason of the fact that she is blind and deaf; nevertheless she is extremely vital and intelligent. It may be that her almost superhuman effort to communicate with a world with which she has such slender contact has done more to enrich her inner spiritual life than all our seeing and hearing has done for us. In like fashion, but in a larger sense, the soul is more than the body and its purposes reach beyond the experiences of this life:

> Though our outward man perish, yet the inward man is renewed day by day . . . for we know that, if our earthly house of this tabernacle were dissolved, we have a building of God, a house not made with hands, eternal in the heavens.[5]

The Larger Life

In all human history men have been lifted up by a strong hope in the continuity of life. There is an inevitability about immortality. It is as though we have an assurance that we are not outward bound, but homeward bound. Even those who live to achieve great age and many distinctions cry out at the last, as did Victor Hugo,

> I have not said a thousandth part of what is in me. When I go down to the grave, I can say with so many others, "I have finished my day's work," but I cannot say, "I have finished my life." Another day's work will begin in the morning. My tomb is not a blind alley; it is a thoroughfare; it closes with the twilight, to open with the dawn.[6]

Life is worth more as a continuous adventure than as a closed affair. We need eternity in which to complete the vision of the hour, for character always falls short of completion here. Idle speculations may work out in a fortunate way for a short time; but the best investments require time and yet more time for vindication. They require eternity. The goal of life cannot be less than the best of life, and if the best of life requires eternity to work out then the goal must look beyond death, and must look with assurance. If, then, the narrow span of life which we know here is lived well only when it is dominated by high purpose, how much more must the larger life beyond require a great conception of purpose to match its significance.

The question of immortality is at the very root of morality. It has been said, and confirmed in history, that when there is no belief in the future life a terrible moral and spiritual decline results. To save us from such a catastrophe the voice of Jesus comes across the ages, "In my Father's house are many mansions; if it were not so, I would have told you."[7] It is in the same spirit that Paul wrote, "And now abideth faith, hope, charity, these three."[8] None of these exist as vague entities apart from persons. These qualities of life demand self-conscious existence after death.

GUARANTEED BY GOD

The arguments which may be marshalled to support our faith in immortality are truly impressive, yet the ultimate fact which guarantees the larger life to us is the fact of God. Because we believe in him we believe in life which continues and in a purpose which endures, a purpose which matches such an opportunity as eternity provides. It is incredible that God would call us into existence, mock us with a crude draught of life, and then let us perish. We repeat the triumphant phrase of the ancient creed, "I believe in life everlasting" as a declaration of confidence in the love of God.

The contemplation of the fact of immortality lifts life to higher levels. It is for this reason that we are commanded of God to let the solemnities of eternity rest on our minds. Yet there is a danger in overemphasis on the glories of the life to come. We have too many evidences of the folly of otherworldliness not to recognize this. Our present life is a significant part of our total life. It must be lived to the full, its problems faced and its lessons learned. This world is the scene of our moral probation. Here character is given its direction. What we need is not to escape from this life, but to find a picture of life as it should be lived here in view of the life which is yet to come. This brings us once more squarely against the fact of our continuing need of God, for no man can fill in this picture for us. Only the Son of God can show us how to live now in anticipation of eternity.

Any conception of the purpose of life which stops short at death fails to satisfy the best and deepest hopes of men. Our purpose is to live now in a way which is wise in view of the larger life which lies beyond death. When we see the need for this, realizing that we are destined for immortality, every passing day takes on new significance. Adversity and setbacks, as well as success and achievement, are seen in a truer light. Issues won or lost may be considered battles, but not the war itself. Life goes beyond old age and death to the good things that pass our present understanding, but which we know God has prepared for those who love him.

Something of this was probably in the mind of Winston Churchill although on a purely temporal level when, at the end of a discouraging stage of World War II, the Allies seemed to be facing certain defeat. Rallying the allied forces, Mr. Churchill called their situation "not the beginning of the end" but the "end of the beginning." His faith proved to be right. In a much more comprehensive sense we must learn to see this life against the fact that God guarantees us larger life, and that the Son of God has died that we might know how to live here so as to be worthy of our great destiny.

1. See Alma 19:82-91.
2. Heb. 3:14, 15.
3. Augustine.
4. Hocking, *The Meaning of Immortality and Human Experience*, Harpers, p. 76.
5. II Cor. 4:16; 5:1.
6. Victor Hugo.
7. John 14:2.
8. I Cor. 13:13.

10 | Purpose and Eternal Life

Wᴇ ʜᴀᴠᴇ sᴇᴇɴ that the life for which we were created is life lived with God and toward God. This life extends into eternity, but it does not wait until death to begin. Eternal life is a life of eternal quality, a life in which the God-given vision and purpose of the ages are brought to bear on the problems and opportunities of the eternal now. To postpone entering into such life is to live on husks when we could be loved and honored in our Father's house.

Eternal life is the life of light and truth. It is enlightened by the quickening influence of the Spirit of God, by the testimony of the years, and by inspired insight into the true nature of our being. It is the life of truth which not only faces the facts but makes room for all the facts — the facts of time and eternity. It is the life in which primary truths are given right of way and in which the facts concerning man's eternal destiny have a bearing on all that we think and say and do.

Tʜᴇ Lɪꜰᴇ ᴏꜰ Jᴇsᴜs

Most of all eternal life is the life of Christ. His life always has been the light of men.[1] He is "the way, the truth, and the *life*."[2] The person in whom the life of Christ abides "hath life; and he that hath not the Son of God hath not life."[3] It could be a terrible thing to live forever with only timebound interests and concerns. Only with the assurance of communion with the eternal Christ and the sharing of his inexhaustible resources does everlasting life become a victory.

It is the purpose of our Father that we shall be in truth his children, adopted sons and daughters, and that the quality of life which was manifest in Jesus shall be manifested in us. The natural man is sometimes referred to as being "carnally minded." His life is motivated by the temporal and temporary values of this earth. The appetites, the possessions, and the creature comforts of the natural man are of major importance to him. If he is wise according to the wisdom of this world he is a good citizen. He recognizes and delights in the beauty of the earth. But the reborn man is "spiritually minded." He has learned to see beyond the turmoil around him, and in spite of the imminence of death he has found life and peace. He has opened his heart and mind and conscience to the indwelling of the spirit of truth. He has surrendered his life to the purpose of God and seeks in love to yield more and more fully to the will of God. As the newborn babe finds life rushing in from all around, so the newborn man in Jesus Christ finds that he is enveloped in a spiritual atmosphere which flows into his life and changes his very being, lifting him up to new heights, giving him a new sense of values, directing him with new motivations.

THE REALITY OF EXPERIENCE

It is difficult to explain to the uninitiated the difference between the two orders of life, the carnal and the spiritual. Our situation is not unlike that of the Venetian traveler, Marco Polo, who came back from Cathay in the fourteenth century and told of the wonders he had seen and the marvelous cities he had visited. Because these things were far beyond the imagination of his untraveled contemporaries, he was accused of lying. Finally everything he tried to say was ridiculed. Upon his deathbed, now past seventy and about to face his God, he was asked to confess his "lies." His last answer was, "I never told the half of it." Nor can the saint tell the half of what it means to live in Christ. What we need is a new language, the language of redemption, which shall express the quality of the life of Christ and yet shall insist that this quality is to be expressed here and now and is not reserved for some otherworldly experience.

In the absence of such a language we are forced back on the realities of our experience, and in this realm we have limited but representative knowledge of what eternal life really is. As we have said it is life turned toward God. We have experienced this life in our personal devotions when we have forgotten our immediate wants and have sought the face of God to learn his purpose for us. Not easily nor quickly — for this world is too much with us — but after genuine and persistent response to the beckoning of our Father, the barriers which have kept us from him have been broken down. We have been visited by the angel of clear vision and have entered into the holy of holies. In this hour of worship many things which have seemed too good to be true are known to be verily so. Such experiences touch our lives with deft and healing fingers. We say with the poet, Masefield: "I have felt a presence that disturbs me with the joy of elevated thought." The hardness of our nature is broken down, and we who were rebellious become willingly obedient as the wonderful love of God dawns upon us. This is not all there is to eternal life, but for the moment we see:

> Life, not the daily toil, but as it is
> Lived in its beauty in eternity,
> Above base aim, beyond our miseries;
> Life that is speed and color and bright bliss,
> And beauty seen and strained for and possessed
> Even as a star forever in the breast.

We have also experienced something of the true nature of eternal life in our corporate worship. Something happens to us and between us when we join in earnest prayer together, when we sing the great hymns of the church, when we listen to the inspired declaration of the great truths of religion, and when we partake together of the emblems of the Lord's Supper or share in the other ordinances of the church. In these experiences we partake of the common life of the body of Christ. Our vision is clarified, our purpose becomes resolute, we become ashamed of our pettiness and insincerity, and in the presence of God we know that we are indeed kin to each other. When we thus lift up our hearts to God and offer our own selves in his service the fire from above brings witness that our offering is acceptable. We say "it is good to be here." We feel in our own souls the richness of eternal life.

The keynote of the worship experience is faith, by which we mean loving confidence in our heavenly Father. Faith is not primarily an intellectual attitude. It is a movement of the heart toward God in loving trust. It is a pledge of fealty, a declaration of loyalty, and a request for orders. We have caught sight of our Captain in the heat of the battle of life. We know him, we love him, we trust him, and the sight of him heartens and refreshes us no matter how weary we were before.

But while it is true that we catch a glimpse of the true meaning of eternal life in these experiences of worship, we cannot retain the vision by remaining in worship overlong. Life calls for spiritual preparation and renewal. But both these terms imply a significant task which lies beyond. And the very quality of the devotions in which we get the feel of eternal life is a prophecy of the importance and necessity of the work for which this experience had prepared the way. If there are to be other experiences of enlightenment in communion

75

then in the intervening days we must use the strength already gained in a new and more vital approach to the problems of daily life.

A LIFE OF EXPANDING DIMENSIONS

It is one of the marks of our inadequacy that we have often thought of eternal life as life stretched out in endless duration. Surely this is not what is meant by our Lord's remarkable declaration that "this is life eternal, that they might know thee the only true God, and Jesus Christ, whom thou has sent."[4] Eternal life involves duration, but only because it first involves quality. Eternal life is life which endures because it has the right to endure. It is life expressed in beautiful relationships, in noble achievements, and in splendid loyalties. It is a life of new dimensions, pushing out constantly in new directions and finding desirable manifestations in new areas of experience. Eternal life is the life of exploration toward God. It is the life which achieves new dominion in areas already controlled, dominion which is for the total good of humanity because it is first of all worshipful and centered in God. It is the life which conquers new continents of experience and proclaims them His.

Eternal life is not an abstract affair. It is not something given as a reward. It is the life of God developed in us as we grow more and more like him. So Paul shared the divine task until he could write, "It pleased God . . . to reveal his Son *in* me."[5] He pleaded with the saints at Philippi, "Let this mind be in you, which was also in Christ Jesus."[6] The whole purpose of his work was to help men and women to invest in those things that endure, making these enduring qualities part of their very selves. He knew that as we truly become Godlike our heavenly Father will entrust us with the opportunities of eternity. We shall then become part of the "church of the firstborn" and shall enjoy the communion of God the Father and of the Son Jesus Christ. The purpose

76

of life will be answered in the quality of our lives when we live and reign with him by reason of being the kind of persons that we were born to be.

Eternal life is life redeemed from pettiness and inconclusiveness by being directed toward a great and worthy end. But such worthy ends as we customarily serve are not elevated enough. Nothing less than the glory of God will do. For there is that in us which requires that our service shall be directed toward the highest and best. In praising God our life is lifted to the highest possible levels.

As soon as we look beneath the surface we find that the inward life itself cannot be pressed or hastened. Our finest virtues are rooted deep. They spring up gradually after many days and nights and have to be watered in all likelihood with many tears. The best fruits of the Spirit ripen slowly and come to perfection almost unaware.

Eternal life is the life of grace. Our first timid ventures on the higher levels of life have given place to the assurance of confidence. We have turned from careful contemplation of every step, and walk boldly because we walk toward our Lord. The inner turmoil of life is quieted. Distractions have lost their power. The stern demands of duty are warmed by the fellowship of love. The stiff awkwardness of spiritual adolescence has passed and we "walk in newness of life," alert, sure and free, for "the law was given through Moses, but life and truth came through Jesus Christ."[7] The law is not forgotten. Its requirements are all fulfilled, but they are fulfilled in glad obedience and not in rebellion or in the awkwardness of merely legal compliance.

The antithesis so often set up between this present life and the mystic glories of eternity is a false contradistinction. Eternal life begins here and now. It is the life of God shared by the faithful and expanding with the years, the life of the kingdom. It stretches forth into a future which blossoms into immortality. If we are mere creatures of a day then awareness of this fact makes it impossible for us to live with dignity and nobility. If we are sons of eternity with an assured and conscious future with God, everything takes on a new and lofty significance. We enlarge and deepen our lives. Our plans for life have a vastness that corresponds to our destiny. When our time comes to pass through the doorway of death this is our Father's business rather than our own. We are prepared, for eternity has already cast its shadow before.

> We are laborers together with God; ye are God's husbandry, ye are God's building. According to the grace of God which is given unto me, as a wise master-builder, I have laid the foundation, and another buildeth thereon. But let every man take heed how he buildeth thereupon. For other foundation can no man lay than that is laid, which is Jesus Christ. Now if any man build upon this foundation gold, silver, precious stones, wood, hay, stubble; every man's work shall be made manifest; for the day shall declare it, because it shall be revealed by fire; and the fire shall try every man's work of what sort it is.[8]

---

1. John 1:4.
2. John 14:6.
3. I John 5:12.
4. John 17:3.
5. Gal. 1:15, 16.
6. Phil. 2:5.
7. John 1:17.
8. I Cor. 3:9-13.

11 | Our Purpose Revealed in the Kingdom

WE ARE LIVING in a time of crisis. On every hand there are evidences that the man-centered social structure which we have fashioned will not stand the strain which we have put upon it. Our philosophers and our historians remind us that all earlier civilizations have collapsed from within, as a result of moral decay, and we can see that situations similar to those which resulted in the downfall of these earlier civilizations are apparent all around us. Mere quickening of our pace along the old road will not save us. What we need is not reform but rebirth. We must die to the selfish, individualistic, sinful lives that we have lived and be born again to a new order of life in which God shall be the center of our ultimate concern. We must learn how to lose our lives in order to save them. We must become in very truth citizens of the kingdom of God.

THE NATURE OF THE KINGDOM

We can only be saved by becoming builders with God of "the city that hath foundations"; and building is not dreaming, it is work. This is the divine method of redeeming society. It begins with individual conversion. It has its root in the change of heart and the uplift of the mind and the redirection of the will which we have called the new birth. But though this change begins in the heart of the individual, by its very nature it immediately reaches out and seeks to include all men. It finds expression in a new order of life in which men seek to live in right relations with each other and are united by a common allegiance to the rule of God.

The kingdom of God is a divine creation. Men have a vital responsibility in the kingdom, but its character and its distinction is that it centers in God. It has been the dream of the prophets from the beginning of time, and Jesus was but carrying forward the prophetic vision to its rightful conclusion when he made John's good news of the kingdom the very heart of his own message.[1] According to Jesus, to have the kingdom is to have all else that matters. The quest for the kingdom is the chief aim of life. We must "seek . . . first to build up the kingdom of God, and to establish his righteousness" before we can hope to have secure hold on the rest of life.[2]

The kingdom life is not merely the refinement of our best thinking or experience, but is God-ordained and God-illuminated. The necessity for it arises out of the very nature of our creation. God has set the kingdom in our hearts. It is because this is so that we are restless until the dream takes shape before our eyes and we see the glory of God manifest in the lives of men.

We have not been given any detailed plans for kingdom building, but have only been invited to acknowledge the kingdom leadership, to share the kingdom spirit, and to pattern our lives according to kingdom principles. It is in working toward the kingdom that the true meaning of the kingdom becomes apparent to us, and we learn what the divine purpose for us really involves. Descriptions of the kingdom have little meaning for us until we launch out in the kingdom enterprise with humility and dedication and according to the best understanding that we have.

The aim of kingdom builders is to discover and promote under God the way of life which will find expression in communities of freedom and justice and equality which are built, as a great church is built, to the glory of God. We cannot create such communities by setting forth a pattern to which everyone must conform. They must grow, and growth is never mechanical. "At the human level the growth of community depends on the free response of men to the needs of their neighbors. What we can do is to discover in human experience those social, economic, political, and cultural conditions which may open the way for the life of free men under God."[3]

There is a sense in which the kingdom of God does not depend on numbers. It exists wherever men acknowledge in their way of life that God is sovereign. In this sense it existed in the person of Jesus. But in a larger sense it is the goal of all rightful endeavor for all mankind. Nations rise and fall, civilizations flourish and pass into decay, but still the movement toward the kingdom continues. By the contributions of obedience, or by the illuminating results of their disobedience, every generation adds something to the structure. We have the promise and hope that the foundation of the kingdom shall be well laid in this dispensation.[4] But though the inclusive purpose of our lives is to build the kingdom of our God and his Christ, we shall never fully succeed until we are clothed with immortality and eternal life and all the generations of the people of God are united in celestial glory.

ASPECTS OF THE KINGDOM

Even as we envision it, the kingdom is so distinct from all other kingdoms with which men are familiar that it is impossible to describe it fully. Knowing this Jesus never attempted a precise definition of the kingdom, but in response to the many questions of his disciples he illustrated its character by parables and word pictures whose meaning is understood only as disciples walk together in the kingdom way. These parables and word pictures do not yield their treasures to the merely curious. But the truth is there for the truly devout. In them Jesus told his disciples that the kingdom is like leaven hidden in a measure of meal;[5] like a hidden treasure;[6] like a merchant seeking a goodly pearl to obtain which he would sell all his other possessions;[7] like growing seed;[8] like ten virgins, five of whom were wise and five foolish.[9] None of these parables exhausts the meaning of the kingdom, but all of them contain some significant germ of truth which only becomes clear with expanding spiritual experience.

A GIFT AND AN ACHIEVEMENT

The kingdom is a gift of the grace of God. In the final analysis it is the gift of himself to those who love and serve him. But his disciples must seek him continuously and must not be satisfied with any lesser gods. The quality of his greatness defies measurement, and we must develop new standards before we begin to sense his true grandeur. It is like this with his kingdom. We cannot see the kingdom, nor can we enter into it, unless we are born of the Spirit of God.[10]

The possibility of the kingdom was given us when we were created to be men of intellect, but also dreamers; men of vision, but also workers; men of earth, yet divinely discontented until we have scaled the heights; and — most surely — when we were called to be disciples. It is a gift which lies buried in the fact of our manhood and our womanhood. It is a gift which opens our eyes to the true purpose of life.

But the kingdom of God makes demands of those who receive it. It is not such a gift as clothes or candy, given solely out of the goodwill of the donor and requiring little or no effort on the part of the recipient. Rather, it is such a gift as the opportunity for education, a gift which cannot be completed without the full cooperation of the receiver. In the case of the kingdom, the very power to respond is a gift of God. But the will to respond is the will of the disciple, and the

82

fullness of his response depends on his love and his faithful endurance.

The building of the kingdom of God is an adventure in the art of practical service. The artist may be born with a touch of genius, but he comes to expertness in the exercise of his gifts only as he develops the power both to see and to portray life. In the art of kingdom building, we must both see kingdom possibilities and then embrace them with joy and fulfill them with love and skill. In a village cemetery in England there is a stone with the simple inscription: "To Thomas Cobb, who mended shoes in this village for forty years to the glory of God." If we assume that the epitaph was well earned, Thomas Cobb was a man of kingdom caliber. That he worked with shoes was comparatively unimportant. That he worked with and for God was all-important. We can be sure that he would not be eulogized as he was if he had not loved God and his fellowmen enough to become a good shoe mender.

It is most unfortunate that we have built up a conflict between the "sacred" and the "secular" and a competition between "material" and "spiritual." This has led us far away from the New Testament ideal of the kingdom of God. In the eyes of Jesus there is but little distinction between these aspects of life. All things which are used for spiritual purposes are spiritual in the sight of God.[11] The kingdom awaits the manifestation of the sons of God. It awaits the coming of a race of men and women who live and work to the glory of God.

THE KINGDOM GROWS

The kingdom is a growing reality. It is a matter of life, not just of addition; of spirit, not just of resources. This was illustrated most profoundly in the advent of the Lord Jesus, who was without possessions and without adornment other than those inherent in his own person. It was his nature and spirit which were important. This is true, also, of the kingdom. It is a seed, small but alive and of tremendous promise.

The kingdom seed grows in two ways: in the extent to which it fills the life of the disciples and in the number of disciples won to allegiance to Christ and the kingdom way. These two are inseparably connected. The kingdom quality of those already won constitutes a major revelation and appeal to others, and those won must themselves grow, or their enlightenment is fruitless. The purpose of God in our creation is fulfilled in this growth in both dedication and testimony.

If and as the kingdom seed proves fruitful, other secondary but important kingdom resources grow also. Of great significance among these are the traditions and patterns of kingdom behavior in which the spirit of the kingdom is embodied. These join the generations and raise kingdom practice above the vision and devotion of any one of them. They go far toward determining the material resources available for day-to-day kingdom endeavor, and supply the frame of reference in which disciples grow in their knowledge of the kingdom and of their own life purpose under God.

A KINGDOM OF BROTHERLY LOVE

The kingdom of God is a kingdom of brothers. Its citizens belong to each other because they are the children of God. Their relation is a family relation, and they are bound to each other by the family spirit and their common participation in the family way of life. This was illustrated in the life of the apostolic church. Hitherto the world had been sharply divided into many social castes. But in the fellowship of the disciples master and bondsman, centurion and common soldier, rich and poor, cultured and unlettered, broke bread together and ministered generously to each other's needs. Moreover, this was not a carefully calculated program. It was the natural flowering of their deep commitment to the Lord Jesus. As they had known him to be, so they sought to be to one another.

We do not know the meaning and the cost and the joys of brotherly love until we make a consistent effort to live on the kingdom level. Yet we cannot believe that the divine purpose in us is that we shall live on any lower plane. We come to know the purpose in our creation as we enter into our best possibilities together under God. We have gone far in building the qualities of individual goodness. We cannot go much further until our group behavior is made to conform more fully to the will of God.

THE FINAL KINGDOM

It is clear that so far we have been discussing the kingdom in terms of its earthly manifestations. There is abundant justification for this in the scriptures.[12] But it is also clear from the scriptures that in its fullest sense Zion, or the kingdom, is celestial glory — the life of the people of God in the presence of the Father and the Son and free from the threat of sin and of death.[13] Moreover, the two are inseparably connected. This is illustrated in the translation of the people of Enoch,[14] and is taught in many New Testament scriptures.

The divine purpose in man is to build the kingdom in and through him so far as this can be done in this present mortal life, to the end that man shall be fitted for the presence of the Father and of the Son.[15] For the fullness of redemption a new heaven and a new earth are required: old things must pass away and all things must become new.[16] But the new heaven and the new earth are not entirely separated from this present earth. They are the sphere of action of those who have partaken of eternal life in this present world, but whose fullness of glory awaits the release from mortality:

> For as many as are led by the Spirit of God, they are the sons of God. For ye have not received the spirit of bondage again to fear; but ye have received the Spirit of adoption; whereby we cry, Abba, Father. The Spirit itself beareth witness with our spirit, that we are the children of God; and if

children, then heirs; heirs of God, and joint heirs with Christ; if so be that we suffer with him, that we may be also glorified together. For I reckon that the sufferings of this present time are not worthy to be named with the glory which shall be revealed in us. For the earnest expectation of the creature waiteth for the manifestation of the sons of God. For the creature was made subject to tribulation not willingly, but by reason of him who hath subjected it in hope; because the creature itself also shall be delivered from the bondage of corruption into the glorious liberty of the children of God. For we know that the whole creation groaneth and travaileth in pain together until now. And not only they, but ourselves also, which have the first fruits of the Spirit, even we ourselves groan within ourselves, waiting for the adoption, to wit, the redemption of our body.[17]

The purpose of God for his children is beyond our comprehension.[18] But we know the direction in which this purpose lies. It is that we shall be fashioned after the image of the Son of God, and that we shall share the glory of his presence with others who are of like heart and mind with us and who shall be gathered together from all the generations and all races of men. The conviction that these things are so lays obligations on us in our present life. The practice here of that which we expect to enjoy in the fullness hereafter is the best preparation for this hereafter, and by the grace of God, the best preparation that we can make for its coming.

---

1. Matt. 4:16, 22; Luke 4:13, 15.
2. Matt. 6:38.
3. Daniel Day Williams, *God's Grace and Man's Hope*, Harper and Brothers, N.Y., p. 167.
4. D. and C. 98:4.
5. Matt. 13:32.
6. Matt. 13:46.
7. Matt. 13:47.
8. Matt. 13:3-7, 20, 31.
9. Matt. 25:1-2.
10. John 3:5.
11. D. and C. 28:8, 9.

12. Ps. 2:8; Isa. 11:9, 42:4; Jer. 23:5; Zech. 14:9; Matt. 5:5; Luke 19:12-19.
13. D. and C. 76:5, I Cor. 15:24-28.
14. D. and C. 36, especially 12 c - 14 e.
15. D. and C. 76:5, John 14:3.
16. Rev. 21:1-5.
17. Rom. 8:14-23. See also Jude 20, 21; Rev. 12:9, 11.
18. I Cor. 2:9, 10.

Part II

The Human Predicament

12 | The Nature of Our Freedom

O NE OF THE GREAT affirmations of the church is that man is by nature a creature of free will. He is "an agent unto himself,"[1] capable of making discriminating choices based on his knowledge of the difference between good and evil.[2] He is made in the image of God in his higher possibilities, not only in his appearance but in his nature. God always respects human freedom. In so doing he respects the personal status which he has given us.

FREE AND CONDITIONED

We are free to choose among alternatives, but we are not free not to choose, for failure to act is itself a decision. And even though we must choose, we are not independent, for we must exercise our freedom in situations which we cannot escape but many aspects of which we have not chosen. There are many illustrations of this fact. We did not choose to be born, yet we hold on to life as a supreme value. We did not choose to be human, yet we must act on the basis of our humanity. We did not choose to be rational rather than to act from instinct alone, but reason we must. We did not choose the time and place of our earthly life, yet these go far to condition our temporal and spiritual opportunity.

Furthermore, as Dr. H. Richard Niebuhr has pointed out,[3] "We make our free decisions not only in such dependence on origins beyond our control, but also in dependence on consequences that are not in our power." The decision of Columbus to sail westward, the decision of Luther to take his stand against the traffic in indulgences, the concern of the boy Joseph over the state of his soul — all these have influenced us mightily. In similar fashion, the decisions which we make, for reasons which are peculiar to us, nevertheless have consequences for people whom we shall never know and in areas which we cannot anticipate.

In light of these considerations it is clear that freedom does not mean an unconditioned power by which a man may choose one course or another with equal ease and without regard to consequences. Indeed, freedom and necessity go hand in hand. Man may reflect on varying goods and goals, and in the light of such reflection he may choose one course of conduct rather than another but, having chosen, he has chosen the results which flow from his decision. And what is true of particular actions is quite true of the total course and purpose of his life. It is the task of the church to persuade and enable man to recognize the privileges and obligations arising out of his freedom. Thus the prophetic word comes to us down the centuries: "Son of man, stand upon thy feet";[4] "Come now, and let us reason together";[5] "Choose you this day."[6]

Freedom is always conditioned. There is no "freedom of the will" as a separate "faculty" in man. We are dealing with feelings and intelligence as well as will when we are concerned with freedom. As Patrick Henry reminded his compeers long ago, "Men of intemperate minds can never be free." We must therefore think of man as a whole, and in relation to his fellows, if we would consider his freedom. His choosing is never unrelated or unmotivated.

AREAS OF LIMITATION

Man's freedom is also limited by his past choices. A

man who has once exercised generous impulses is likely to continue in the mood of generosity, his basic nature being reinforced by habit. A man who was once free to live cleanly may now find that dirty thoughts, at first entertained casually, have moved in and intend to stay. By repeated choices put forth in a given direction the course of life may become so confirmed in good or in evil that men are "the servants of righteousness"[7] or the bond "servant of sin."[8]

Habit is choice which persists and grows stronger as like choices are added to it. It influences all subsequent action. Both our individual lives and the social order are thus conditioned. Both are permeated with selfishness. The evils of the yesterdays live on in our ungodly personal habits and social practices. We are in the situation which Paul described when he wrote:

> When I would do good evil was present with me; for I delight in the law of God after the inward man. And now I see another law, even the commandment of Christ, and it is imprinted in my mind. But my members are warring against the law of my mind, and bringing me into captivity to the law of sin which is in my members. . . . O wretched man that I am! Who shall deliver me from the body of this death?[9]

In very truth a man who is in bondage to sin which has made it impossible for him to see straight or to feel straight or to act straight can only be free if he is born again.[10]

On careful thought it is also clear that man's freedom is impaired by his preoccupations and his faulty insight. There can be no true choice without awareness of the alternatives. A man in a procession tends to turn with the procession regardless of the better routes that he passes by. A man intent on pursuing an unworthy objective may be oblivious to the claims of a more worthy one. A man who has never cultivated his artistic possibilities may pass by beauty unaware. Unless the Lord had opened his eyes, the young man would never have beheld the mountain full of horses and chariots of fire round about Elisha.[11]

Then, too, man's freedom is limited by his situation among his fellows. He does not live alone. He can only come to full selfhood as he lives and grows among other men — stimulating them and being stimulated by them. In the course of this interaction he cannot forever act with a view to his own narrowly conceived well-being. Whether he wants to do so or not, he must give some attention to the desires of others and, in time, to their rights. Much of our law is concerned with specifying these rights in such fashion that the rules are no longer matters for argument but, rather, for agreement. Yet there always remains a vast area of human conduct in which personal choices have to be made, in which human values and well-being are involved. In these areas moral and spiritual factors are particularly important.

FREEDOM, AGENCY, AND RESPONSIBILITY

Despite the limitations on man's freedom, he is truly free. While it is not true that a man born in the slums or in some undeveloped country is as free as a man born in suburban United States, it is true that such a man has a large measure of freedom, and his character is determined by the use he makes of that freedom. The endless variety and unpredictability of life as we know it are proofs of the reality of that freedom, supporting what we know from our own consideration of our situation. Man is no mere passive resultant of the forces which impinge on his life; he is a free actor in his world. If he will he can make discriminating choices. Furthermore, he can transcend the moment and choose long-range goals and commit himself to a deliberately chosen way of life. Finally, and more important than anything else, he can adopt for himself a purpose higher than his own, and partake of a Spirit which enables him to transcend limitations which would otherwise make his seeming freedom a mockery.

This higher freedom — freedom within accepted obligations and responsibilities — is illustrated in a sound marriage. In such a marriage complete mutual trust is set against the powerful wants centering in the chance excitements of the world and the imperious instincts of sex. How wise, therefore, are those who put and keep their marriage relationship under a vow, a vow made not merely to one another but also to a Higher Will to which both feel that they owe loyalty and which preserves their loyalty to each other. In such a marriage the vow is not a limitation and an indication of bondage. On the contrary, it is the doorway to freedom. "There is no real infringement of agency when the compulsive force is attraction."[12]

The union of freedom and restraint is most fully expressed in the idea of predestination. Many modern thinkers are repelled by this doctrine because it has been so taught that it seems to mock the reality of freedom. But there is a sense in which the idea of predestination is inescapable, for its intention is to affirm the purpose of God behind creation, the destiny toward which our lives have been pointed from the beginning. Predestination in this sense is evident all around us. As the purpose of the cabinetmaker determined the form and structure of the table which he has made, so also has the purpose of our heavenly Father determined our nature and endowment, and the ends we are shaped to serve. We have agency which is denied to such an immaterial thing as a table, but this agency operates as it is intended within the framework of our creation. Man is predestined, but not in such fashion as to destroy his power of self-determination. He is like a swimmer who is held up by the water, but who must also make an effort of his own if he expects to swim.

Throughout this discussion we have been concerned with moral freedom as though it were synonymous with agency.

94

Yet always the note of obligation creeps in. When we say that a man is "an agent unto himself," we mean, primarily, that he can determine for himself his attitude toward life and all that life offers him or does to him, but that his decision is a responsible one. A created being who is an "agent unto himself" is under moral obligation to fulfill the purpose of his creation. In the nature of things, this purpose is the purpose of his Creator; it is a purpose which has already written into his being his rightful ends as well as his natural beginnings. The Hebrew young men might be faced with the fiery furnace if they stood true to their faith, but they still had the power to say, "We will not worship the golden image." Joseph S. Carter, Jr., stated his own faith in this regard, and at the same time challenged his Negro brethren, when he wrote:

Brother, come!
And let us go unto our God.
And when we stand before him
I shall say —
"Lord, I do not hate;
I am hated.
I scourge no one!
I am scourged.
I covet no lands;
My lands are coveted.
I mock no peoples;
My peoples are mocked."
And, Brother, what shall you say?[13]

FREEDOM AND SOCIAL RESPONSIBILITY

One of the disturbing phenomena of our day is the way in which the sense of personal responsibility is coming to be a diminishing factor in determining human conduct. It is impossible to pinpoint all the reasons for this, but one of them is the current overemphasis on the role of social forces in the shaping of our lives. Man tends to be regarded more and more as an infinitesimal fragment of the body politic rather than as an individual who is of priceless value in himself and whose distinctive qualities are added to this value.

Doctor L. P. Jacks has pointed out that we need to recognize our relation to and our responsibility in regard to the subhuman creation. He says:

> We human beings are apt to think our race the only object in creation that really matters. We have developed a kind of class-consciousness in presence of the universe. The human race is all-important in its own eyes: Nature is there to be ruled by us; her forces were meant to turn our wheels; her materials to be exploited for our enrichment; her laws to provide for our comfort; and the very stars in their courses must be yoked to our wagons. We still have to learn that the human race is tolerated in the universe only on strict condition of good behavior. If we neglect our citizenship there, or think that we can play fast and loose with the laws that are written there, laws that were not voted into existence by us, those other citizenships will come to grief. This human class-consciousness in presence of the rest of the universe is not a good thing. It is a dangerous thing. Unless we bear that in mind, our study of the rights and duties of the citizen is not worthwhile.[14]

Guiseppe Mazzini, the great Italian patriot, lifted this to the plane of our common brotherhood when he wrote to his compatriots a hundred years ago:

> Generally speaking, you cannot, even if you would, separate your life from that of humanity; you live in it, by it, for it. I charge you then, O my brothers, by your duty and by your own interest not to forget that your first duties—duties without fulfilling which you cannot hope to fulfill those owed to family and country—are to humanity. You are all brothers. Ask yourselves whenever you do an action in the sphere of your country, or your family, if what I am doing were done by all and for all, would it advantage or injure humanity? And if your conscience answers, it would injure humanity, desist; desist, even if it seems to you that an immediate advantage for your country or your family would ensue from your action. Be apostles of this faith, apostles of the brotherhood of nations, and of the unity of the human race.[15]

The divine purpose in us is that, being free and yet responsible, we shall choose to serve God and our fellows. This is not a single choice. It is a way of life.

---

1. D. and C. 28:9 b. See also 37:2 b, 101:2 f.
2. Gen. 6:58, I.V.; Hel. 5:85, 86.
3. H. Richard Niebuhr, *Christ and Culture* (New York: Harper & Brothers, 1951), p. 250.
4. Ezek. 2:1.
5. Isa. 1:18.
6. Josh. 24:15.
7. Rom. 6:15-23.
8. John 8:31-36.
9. Rom. 7:23-26.
10. John 3:5.
11. II Kings 6:17.
12. Dewar and Hudson, *Christian Morals* (Hodder and Stoughton), p. 31.
13. Quoted from *Great Companions*, 1:391, The Beacon Press.
14. From his *Constructive Citizenship*.
15. From his *Duties of Man*.

13 | Agency and Sin

THE CENTRAL HUMAN tragedy, in which every one of us is involved, is that men act as though they were their own creators, and use their God-given powers irresponsibly. It is difficult for ordinary men to see this, but the prophets have both seen and declared it. Ezekiel put it this way:

> Then said I unto them, Cast ye away every man the abominations of his eyes, and defile not yourselves with the idols of Egypt; I am the Lord your God. But they rebelled against me, and would not hearken unto me; they did not every man cast away the abominations of their eyes, neither did they forsake the idols of Egypt. . . . Wherefore . . . I polluted them in their own gifts.[1]

The latter-day prophet said:

> They seek not the Lord to establish his righteousness, but every man walketh in his own way, and after the image of his own god, whose image is in the likeness of the world, and whose substance is that of an idol, which waxeth old and shall perish in Babylon, even Babylon the great, which shall fall.[2]

At the heart of all man's sinning is his tendency to think and act as though he were God, putting himself instead of God in the center of his world. Only a creature made in the image of God could do this. As a consequence, his life is off-center, and the tremendous possibilities which would be

98

his as a child of God go unrealized because he is in bondage to himself. The temptation to which Adam and Eve listened was not primarily a physical matter; it actually meant, "Ye shall be as gods."[3]

When finite men, whose true being and destiny consists in loyal obedience to infinite goodness, transgress the will of their Creator and set themselves against the constituted order of life, the most dire consequences follow. The Greeks spoke about "Nemesis" and the "Furies" which trailed the steps of transgressors. The Hebrews proclaimed that "the stars in their courses fought against Siser," that is, against the violator of elemental righteousness.

It has been said that "world history is world judgment." It is the story of the ripening satisfactions which have followed obedience to the order of our being, and the tragedy which has followed disobedience. It gives many illustrations of the fact that when any human good is clutched and cherished and put in place of the Sovereign Good this seeming good utterly fails those who put their trust in it. Dr. John A. Mackay has said:

> When science is hailed as the world savior, it produces a weapon which creates world gloom and foreshadows world destruction. When civilization is pursued as an end in itself, a psychology is produced in the "civilized," which makes it difficult for civilization to maintain itself. The poetic insight of Francis Thompson is literally true on the plane of world history, "All things forsake thee, who forsaketh me."[4]

COMPLACENCY

One of the major difficulties which confronts our heavenly Father in his attempt to induce us to fulfill the purpose of our creation is our complacency with our own sins. It is not desirable that we shall dwell morbidly on the negative aspects of life. But it is important that we shall know our true situation, and shall face squarely the major reasons for our

99

moral and spiritual ineptitude. We must face sin rather than ignore it. Denying the fact of sin is like denying the fact of disease. Sin, like cancer, must be recognized, diagnosed, and treated, or it will kill.

No bridge builder can hope to succeed when he ignores the steady downward pull of gravity and shuts his eyes to the destructive power of the flood beneath, nor can the builder of a life succeed if he shuts his eyes to the significance of sin. If we would build our lives securely, we must face the facts of life squarely, and one of these facts is that sin brings sickness and pain and death.

There are many wide differences of belief between the various Christian denominations, but they are united in their testimony to the fact of sin and the possibility of its forgiveness. Distrust any part of theology, Martin Luther has said, that cannot be reduced to the forgiveness of our sins. Poverty, ignorance, immorality, disease, war, industrial and political slavery — how hateful and how persistent they are! How arrogantly they claim the consideration of men and women who would build a better world. But out of the host of symptomatic ills which play upon humanity, the Christian takes the source and strength of them all, sin, and singles it out for annihilation. Attack sin and the problems of humanity are attacked at the root.

> There is just one great affirmation about human life and society that is big enough, radical enough, true enough, to go into the creed of Christians, and that is, "I believe in getting rid of sin." Sin is the one root of evil; lessen that, and real progress is made. Get rid of that, and other evils will disappear. The Christian is concerned about sin, nothing less, nothing lighter. Life is wrong because men do wrong, and even more because men are wrong. Sin is the one evil about which we need to get aroused, against which we need to direct all our forces.[5]

The way to a better world is to join with God in the fight against sin.

100

When we think about sin from the Christian viewpoint, it is apparent that if we are to know what is wrong with man we must first understand what a "true and proper" man is: what man would be like if he were without sin. By the grace of God we have such a standard in the person of the Lord Jesus Christ.[6] Any who are seriously concerned can now see the true nature of sin by contrast with the life of compassionate love lived by Jesus. Under his guidance we now see and measure sin by its unlikeness to the spirit of the Master. Since Jesus Christ has been here, the hues of sin have grown darker and more distinct. As we come to know Jesus and to live with him, we can see sin more clearly and begin to understand how it looks to God. As we do this we realize that sin is life lived independently of God. The sinner puts something, either himself or the world, in the place which rightly belongs to Divinity. Sin is in fact godlessness; it is acting as though we wished for the moment and for this particular experience God did not have to be taken into account.

The difficulty with many of the definitions of sin is that they fail to paint sin in its true perspective because they fail to set it forth against this background of the unfailing love of God revealed by Jesus. Sin takes on a more personal significance when we consider it in light of what God has done for us. This is one of the things that Jesus sought to do when he told the story of the Prodigal Son. Against such a background we can see sin as being "estrangement from our Father," "treason against the love of God," and "a great betrayal of divine trust." It includes both omission and commission, both failing to do what we ought to do and doing what we ought not to do. But it includes both of these because we are away from God, and are living apart from him when we might live with him.

101

Originally the word "sin" meant a missing of the mark. It is related to the English word "wrong" which means "wrung" or "twisted." From this it has come to indicate conduct and character which do not conform to the standards set by God. Sinful conduct is therefore the action of a wrung and twisted and crooked life, a life that is not square with the life and purpose of God.

Sin should be carefully distinguished from error or ignorance. Plato felt that man's problem was a lack of knowledge, that man does wrong merely because he does not know the right. But sin is infinitely worse and cuts far deeper into the soul than ignorance. Our difficulty does not lie primarily in our many mistakes and misunderstandings, but in our willfulness. Our problem is not in what we do not know as much as it is in what we do know. It is the informed, enlightened man that is on the edge of annihilating himself.

The continued problem of sin is not that we have missed the path but that we have chosen other paths. We are in transgression—trespassers paying little heed to the boundary line marking the distinction between right and wrong. Through blindness and through perversity we are wandering off the highway when we should be pressing forward on our Father's business. We are the modern Jonahs, who are sailing toward Tarshish when we know in our hearts that we should be bound for Ninevah.

We would not be pessimistic. There is much of good in man, as well as much of evil — original righteousness as well as original sin. This we have affirmed. But it is important that we recognize sin to be what it is, in all its dark horror. Sin is not "good in the making." It does not call for improvement, but rather for destruction. Sin is not "ignorance" which can be eradicated by education. It cannot be destroyed by inventing other names for it, because it is a disease of the soul as virulent and as harmful as leprosy. It is not something outside of us which appeals to us; it has become part of our very selves. Error, misfortune, and similar ills come from without, but sin reigns within. It is first of all an attitude of heart and mind alienated from God, and from this attitude spring all the outward evidences of our ungodliness. "Sin is a sinner sinning." Recognizing this, "the Son of God was manifested, that he might destroy the works of the devil."[7]

When William Temple was a student at Oxford he listened to a visiting American preacher bear down on the theme: "Though your sins be as scarlet, they shall be as white as snow." Temple said to a friend, "My sins are not scarlet, they are gray — all gray." What Temple missed and what all of us so often fail to take into consideration is the sin of pride and rebellion that lies at the heart of our self-centered lives, which makes our predicament more scarlet than we wish to believe.

The note of estrangement and of rebellion against God is strongly emphasized in modern revelation: "The rebellious shall be pierced with much sorrow,"[8] and, later,

> They who go forth, bearing these tidings unto the inhabitants of the earth, to them is power given to seal, both on earth and in heaven, *the unbelieving and rebellious.*[9]

And, still later,

> Let the wicked take heed, and let the rebellious fear and tremble; and let the unbelieving hold their lips.[10]

In the words of P. T. Forsyth, "As a race we are not stray sheep, or wandering prodigals merely; we are rebels taken with weapons in our hands."

What we have seen is expressed by the apostle Paul in the letter to the Roman saints: "Whatsoever is not of faith is sin."[11] It is difficult to find a more inclusive definition, or

103

one which bears more clearly on the purpose of our lives in answering the purpose of God in our creation. According to the apostle, any act which is not rooted and grounded in confident trust and commitment to God is sinful.

How Men Sin

In all the things which Jesus called sinful there is a basic element of selfishness. The sinner grasps things for himself regardless of the will of God; or he asserts himself aggressively, and refuses to live helpfully in the community as one whose life and happiness is wrapped up in that of his fellows; or he may allow self-righteousness to foul the springs of all he does. Behind this hard note in the teaching of Jesus, and giving it meaning, lies the sense of high calling. The sinner is the grasping, self-centered individual who has turned his back on God's purpose and set at naught the divine counsel.

Such sin is manifested in a multiplicity of ways with which we have no primary concern in this study; but we shall be helped if we face the fact that specific areas of sinfulness are all manifestations of attitudes which reflect our rebellion and — what is the same thing — our selfishness. The most prevalent of these is the refusal of so many to recognize life as a divinely ordained means to a divinely envisioned end. For the Christian the chief end of man is to glorify God — to cooperate in the fulfillment of the divine purpose in him — and when he fails or refuses to point his efforts in this direction with some sense of urgent obligation he has missed his mark in life, and sin lies at his door. It is this fact which explains the emphasis which Jesus laid on motive and intention rather than on specific outward acts. If a man, in his heart, is not right with God, not set on fulfilling the purpose of God in his life, he is not right at any point in his life. "I have set the Lord always before me," says the Psalmist.[12]

It is only when self-consciousness begins with the growing power of insight and of choice that we find the possibility of sin. The church has emphasized this through its concern that children shall not be baptized until they have "come to the age of accountability." But this very provision indicates that there is an obligation of more elevated choice which goes with the sharpening of intelligence. This is illustrated in a suggestion of the late Edward Grubb.[13] He says, suppose a salmon were to become intelligent and to question why it should suffer buffeting and bruises in the attempt to breast the torrent and surmount the rocks, asking, "Why should I take all this trouble? Why not swim downstream to the sea, where there is such abundance of food?" To ask this and to do this would be sin, made possible only through the salmon's assertion of his right of self-determination. Sin is a voluntary choosing of the easy path of self-indulgence, contrary to the law of my being. It is self-assertion against the divine ordering of the world.

Our word "virtue" is derived from the Latin "virtus," which denotes vigor and valor and efficiency. What falls short of virtue is sin. "He that is not with me, is against me."[14] The apathy and spiritual sluggishness of those who have allowed their lives to be hampered by jealousies and vindictiveness and petty lying sometimes seems a greater obstacle to the advancement of the kingdom of God than the known evil of the few. All too frequently the tepid goodness of nominally Christian men is totally unwelcome to God, who has no use for those who are neither hot nor cold.[15] "He was not a bad man," we read of Jean-Christophe's father, "but a half-good man, which is perhaps worse."

There are sins at every level of life, sins of omission and sins of commission. Some of these sins, particularly those of omission, being yielded to, make sure that we shall never be faced with temptations which belong to higher levels. An example is that drunkenness saves the drunkard from the temptation of spiritual pride which may well beset another man who is devout but who is inclined to be a Pharisee.

Because of this we cannot rightfully say that sin is simply falling below a fixed standard of conduct, even though we can list sins which tend to beset us at any level. Sin is any kind of disloyalty, missing any divinely designated mark at which we should be pointing; it is any manifestation of selfishness which indicates that we are not fulfilling the divine purpose in us.

THE FIGHT AGAINST SIN

The work of righteousness is not complete when we become aware of ourselves as sinners, but nevertheless the realization of our sinfulness is imperative as a prelude to sharing the joy and power of forgiveness. Isaiah was not a morbid man. He was a man of political acumen and spiritual vigor who was respected by the leaders of his people and who has been a major force for righteousness down the succeeding centuries. But read the moving account of vision of the glory of God[16] and note the importance he places on his need of forgiveness. Paul, too, could hold his own in any company, yet his sense of the awfulness of sin and the wonder of divine forgiveness ran through every letter he wrote.[17] John Wesley was the most significant figure in the history of eighteenth-century England. He did more for the English people of his generation than any statesman or soldier of his time, and he did it by reawakening in the common people a sense of the majesty of God and of the consequent awfulness of sin. It was no accident that men such as these stood out among their fellows. They did so because they saw life and its issues as these truly are. They sought to bring their lives into line with the purpose of God, and to do this the first step was to recognize that they were out of line.

When it is allowed to become an end in itself, the sense of sin is a desperate thing; but as a step toward our enlightenment by the truth, its very pain is an evidence of life, and its humiliation is a prophecy of coming growth.

106

There is a passage in an old story that puts the truth very simply and very beautifully. According to this story a woman was greatly troubled by her sins and talked with a wise old minister about them. The minister told her:

> You have sinned, and suffered for your sins. You have asked your heavenly Father to forgive you, and he has forgiven you. But still you suffer. Woman, be thankful that you can suffer. The worst trouble in the world is the trouble that does not know God, and so does not suffer. Without such knowledge there is no suffering. The sense of sin in the soul is the apprehension of Almighty God.[18]

The divine purpose for men is life abundant. In the New Testament the inclusive word for sin — which is action contrary to the richness of life — is death. Sin is the refusal of life, and death is not merely the consequence of such refusal but is existence in which this refusal is a controlling factor. Paul apparently had this in mind when he cried for deliverance "from the body of this death."[19] For him to set the mind on the flesh was death, just as to set the mind on the Spirit was life. He who does not love remains in death. A man's higher possibilities are never born in him if he continues in sin, and those which he has already glimpsed and begun to experience are killed when sin is allowed to take the reins.

1. Ezekiel 20:7, 8, 25.
2. D. and C. 1:3 d, e.
3. Gen. 3:10.
4. *God's Order,* The Macmillan Company, p. 33.
5. W. P. Merrill, *The Common Creed of Christians* (Westwood, N.J.: Fleming H. Revell Co.), p. 122.
6. John 8:46.
7. I John 3:8.
8. D. and C. 1:1 c.
9. D. and C. 1:2 c.
10. D. and C. 63:2 b.
11. Rom. 14:23; also I John 3:4; 5:17.
12. Psalm 16:8.

13. In his *Religion of Experience,* Headly Bros., p. 157.
14. Luke 11:24.
15. Rev. 3:15, 16.
16. Isa. 6:1-8.
17. I Tim. 1:15.
18. Margaret Deland, *Old Chester Tales,* p. 84.
19. Rom. 7:26.

14 Original Sin

MEN ARE BORN FREE. This freedom is real, but it is relative and not absolute. A major limitation under which we all labor is that we come into the world with a definite tendency to choose evil; we seem to be "bent to backsliding."[1] We do not find it as easy to do right as it is to drift into indolence, indulgence, selfishness, and worse. Pursuit of the higher virtues requires effort; it is a movement upstream. This is only partly explained by the fact that achievement of the heights requires the development of new insights and powers. It also involves the subjugation of self-centered impulses which appear to be part of our very nature.

Because of this aspect of our existence, from the time of St. Augustine down to today there have been attempts to show how the sin of our first parents has made all human beings guilty sinners in the eyes of God. This concept has been called "original sin," although the term is nonbiblical. In one form or another the concept has become a part of Christian thought. *The New England Primer* read:

> "In Adam's fall
> We sinned all."

And according to this point of view:

> "Hell is crammed
> With infants damned
> Without a day of grace."

109

It is significant that no such teaching as described above is to be found in the scriptures. The Book of Mormon is very clear on the subject of the innocence of children.[2]

TOTAL DEPRAVITY

For many, the doctrine of original sin has been closely associated with that of total depravity. This doctrine, as represented by Augustine and Calvin, held that the whole creation was perfectly good, including man, but that when Adam sinned he radically changed the situation. His nature, the theory holds, was changed from wholly good to wholly evil. This evil nature was passed on from Adam to every one of his descendants, who were held to have sinned in him as their progenitor and representative and "federal head." As the Westminster Confession put it: "We are utterly indisposed, disabled, and made opposite to all good, and wholly inclined to all evil."

Calvin headed the third chapter of the second book of his *Institutes*: "Everything proceeding from the corrupt nature of man damnable." As he put it,

> The hydra lurks in every breast. For as a body, while it contains and fosters the cause and matter of disease, cannot be called healthy, although pain is not actually felt; so a soul, while teeming with such seeds of vice, cannot be called saved. This similitude, however, does not apply throughout. In a body, however morbid, the functions of life are performed; but the soul, when plunged into the deadly abyss [of sin], not only labors under vice, but is altogether devoid of good.[3]

A modern revival of Calvinism has been initiated by Karl Barth, who has used such an expression as "the darkness which is man" and has referred to our human body as "this stinking sack." But many of the spiritual descendants of Calvin now know that the doctrine of total depravity is contrary to the biblical teaching concerning man. The narrative in Genesis indicates no sharp and complete change from total goodness to total depravity but, rather, pictures both Adam and Eve as sufficiently aware of their situation to hide from God. Their shame testified to their awareness of shortcoming, and this is a long way from total lack of capacity for knowing God or for responding to him.

The doctrine of agency is squarely opposed to the doctrine of total depravity. Affirmation of our moral freedom is in line with both the Old and the New Testaments and with other Restoration scriptures which assume the presence in all men of some capacity for response to the call of God. "There is a spirit in man; and the inspiration of the Almighty giveth them understanding."[4] God has made us in his image and this image, though marred, has never been completely defaced.

THE FALL

Theories concerning original sin and total depravity have also been closely associated with the idea of the fall of man. The story in Genesis tells that Adam was expressly forbidden to eat of the tree of the knowledge of good and evil, but at the same time was assured that the choice lay with him.[5]

It may be because we are so like Adam that we find it hard to realize how he could really be a man without tasting the fruit of that tree, and so asserting his freedom of action. We have never known self-consciousness to be developed except through conflict — the assertion of our selves against other selves and the pursuit of ends which seem good to us in preference to ends which others may recommend to us. But we do have available to us a picture showing the general tone of what might have happened if Adam had freely chosen to obey his Creator. This picture is furnished to us in the life of the Lord Jesus Christ, who came from heaven not to do his own will but the will of Him that sent him, and who has shown us that obedience is a way of life for free men.[6] Manliness at its best is greatly admired among men, especially the manly men, but it is not godliness. And, no matter what knowledge and skill they control, men as men cannot and do not determine their own destiny.

The story of the fall of man is significant for every one of the children of Adam, for it expresses truths of vital importance to all of us. It tells us that God has given us our freedom and invites us to walk in his way with the full consent of heart and mind and conscience. It says that we have misused the freedom which God has given us by refusing to accept his counsel and walk in his way. This refusal is dramatized in the story found in Genesis, and the story is true to what happened at the beginning and also to what happens in every generation. It has been said that every new generation is a new invasion of barbarians. And the story of the fall says that our choice of sin brings consequences in its train, as does the choice of good. But the superficially apparent results are not the most significant ones. These lie in the character which is shaped by obedience or disobedience, and in the fellowship which is determined by this character.

ORIGINAL SIN

We come now to consider what guidance there may be for us in the idea of original sin modified by what we have already considered.

First of all, the doctrine of original sin emphasizes a fact about all mankind — that we are self-willed and proud of it. William Ernest Henley spoke for many of us in his bravely defiant poem "Invictus":

> Out of the night that covers me,
>   Black as the Pit from pole to pole,
> I thank whatever gods may be
>   For my unconquerable soul.
>
>   .   .   .
>
> It matters not how strait the gate,
>   How charged with punishments the scroll,
> I am the master of my fate;
>   I am the captain of my soul.[7]

112

Despite the fact that I have heard "Invictus" sung in our churches, and its sentiments applauded by those who should have known better, it is only in a secondary and permissive sense that we are the masters of our fate, that we are captains of our souls. But for the grace of God we have neither existence nor destiny. To act as though we have is to rebel against the facts of creation and Providence. It is sin, and this sin is characteristic of men as we know them. Frederic Amiel wrote in his diary,

> An instinct of revolt, an enemy of all law, a rebel which will stoop to no yoke, not even that of reason, duty and wisdom. This element in us is the root of all sin.[8]

The New Testament points out this native tendency toward evil very clearly, stating that "by one man sin entered into the world, . . . for as by one man's disobedience many were made sinners, so by the obedience of one shall many be made righteous,"[9] and that we are "by nature the children of wrath."[10] This doctrine is also taught in the Book of Mormon[11] and in the Doctrine and Covenants.[12] And it is also taught in experience, for despite its somber tone, the fact of the transmission of the tendency to evil is so apparent as to be undeniable.

Another truth of the doctrine of original sin is that no matter how eager Adam and Eve may have been later to face the responsibility for their sins, it was impossible for them to do so completely. By the simple fact of their parenthood they were knit to all future generations. When they sinned, the law which ties the generations together began to tie men together for evil as well as for good. It was not the will of God that this should be so. It was his will that the generations should be united for good. But the law which was designed to work for our salvation has been disordered by the willfulness of the first and following generations, and has become a primary factor in our present frustration.

113

Our heavenly Father wants us to know this. Through the experience of our progenitors and through our own, He is seeking to teach us that no man can escape from his forebears or from his children. Human lives are shaped by the prevailing tones of prior generations and by the hopes of the living for those who shall come after. When the first generation sinned all future generations were burdened by their sin; and when contemporary generations sin, all future generations are thereby burdened. Consider our heritage from World War II. Much of the noblest work of those who had gone before was destroyed and many of their dearest hopes were blasted; generations who might have been born were denied life, or were started out in life with a burden of debt and hatred and fear; war itself, an ancient enemy of mankind, was given a new lease on life. Beyond all question, the burden of sin carries on from generation to generation.

In a lecture given in Kansas City in April, 1963, Dr. Arnold Toynbee, the eminent historian, tried to depict the man of the future looking back on this first generation of men of the space age. Dr. Toynbee pointed out what a marvelous breakthrough we achieved before the space age could be possible. And then he lamented that because the selfishness and self-will of men of the last stages of the pre-space-age was ill-suited to the new order, the threats of that new order were incalculably multiplied and its benefits greatly delayed.

SOCIAL SOLIDARITY

The doctrine of original sin has another meaning for us in that it stands for the fact that mankind shares responsibility for social evils. Men are not individuals standing apart from the larger community. We belong in the community, and share the current way of life with its widespread denial of genuine world brotherhood. We need to be penitent and humbled as we envision the holiness of the Lord, not only because our own lips are unclean, but also because we dwell

114

"in the midst of a people of unclean lips" whose words and ways we share.[13]

A man who does not wish to be identified with his immediate family or nation may change his name or migrate to another country, but, as the scriptures make clear, that man cannot escape his identification with mankind. "No man is an island." In a very real sense what happens to one of a group happens to the group as a whole. Nor can we immediately and decisively change the situation of which we are part. Only God can do that, and he will not do it in ways which infringe on our freedom. Without his forgiveness and his patient guidance in the way of the kingdom the weight of our social responsibility might be too much to bear for those who have eyes to see and the heart to understand.

THE REALITY OF REDEMPTION

There are those who resent very deeply the limitations on freedom imposed by the facts indicated in our study of original sin. It does not seem fair to them that a child should come into the world burdened by the weight of the wrongdoing of his progenitors and of mankind in general. But it should be clear that this is not a matter of guilt, but of fact. And it is unavoidable. It is a corollary of our racial solidarity, as unavoidable as the fact that the same street may lead to or from town. It is not for us to fight against the fact of our kinship down the generations. This is how God has made us, and there is no basis for resentment of his plan since we have never known any other and must stand away from all that we have known to even begin to imagine any other. If we are truly Christian we shall accept the nature of our creation with gratitude and, if we do, the fact of our kinship is still written deep. We belong together, even as we belong to God. If we learn by bitter experience that "in Adam all die"[14] we can also learn from joyous association with our Master that in Christ shall all men be "made alive."

When we come to understand the far-reaching consequences of our sinning, the grace of God works in us to make this insight an inducement toward right doing. But we cannot achieve this insight by ourselves. Left to ourselves, it takes a world war to reveal the foolishness of our talk of inevitable progress toward the "higher life." But under the guidance of the Holy Spirit we realize that our only salvation is to be "strong in the Lord, and in the power of his might."[15] This is the foundation of our humility and of our hope.

Original sin is not our fault, but it is our problem. It becomes our fault only when we add to it and so increase the burden of those who follow after us. Our responsible relation to the problem lies in the fact that life is so organized that we belong together and that both the good and the evil which we do live after us. This fact confronts every saint and every sinner with a requirement which cannot be escaped.

---

1. Hos. 11:7.
2. See Moroni 8:9-13.
3. *Institutes,* Calvin, II, iii, a.
4. Job 32:8.
5. Gen. 2:20-22, I.V.
6. Phil. 2:8; Mark 14:36; John 6:38, 15:10; Rom. 5:19; Heb. 5:8.
7. *Masterpieces of Religious Verse,* No. 1848.
8. *Amiel's Journal* (February 23, 1870), Vol. II:55.
9. Rom. 5:12, 19.
10. Eph. 2:3.
11. II Nephi 1:70; Mosiah 1:119; 8:73-78; Helaman 5:70, 71; Alma 19:75.
12. Doctrine and Covenants 17:4.
13. Isa. 6:5.
14. I Cor. 15:22.
15. Eph. 6:10.

15 | Your Sin and Mine

THERE IS A WIDESPREAD agreement among Christians that the great enemy of mankind is sin. Yet many of us all the time, and all of us much of the time, merely recognize this to be a fact. Our convictions about sin are not deep enough or colorful enough to send us forth on any crusades. Although we may be bitterly ashamed when our private transgressions are brought to light, we conform in a general way to the standards of our times without undue questioning. The characteristic work of sin in most of us has been to blind us to the sinfulness of our sinning; but if we are to fulfill the purpose of God in our creation, something must happen to alert us to the realization of what sin is and what sin does, and to a sense of responsibility because of these facts. We must recognize sin in its true colors and act accordingly.

In the final analysis sin and righteousness are matters of the spirit. Outward acts are important, but attitudes of heart and mind are even more important, for the outward acts come from these inner attitudes:

> From within, out of the hearts of men, proceed evil thoughts, adulteries, fornications, murders, thefts, covetousness, wickedness, deceit, lasciviousness, an evil eye, blasphemy, pride, foolishness; all these evil things come from within, and defile the man.[1]

117

Knowing these things, it is amazing that we do not give more time and more thought and more earnest endeavor to the cultivation of our souls, but in these modern luxurious times we are too busily occupied with good things to give attention to the best things. In many a life the worst enemy of the best has proved to be the second best.

The amazing feats of imagination which underly our remarkable progress in the physical realm have little counterpart on the spiritual level. Many of us take it for granted that because we enjoy the advantages of modern times we are therefore more intelligent and live more creatively than our grandfathers did. This would be very difficult to prove. The Western nations have more ideas and a more highly perfected technology than we have the ability to realize and assimilate. A Sunday paper alone contains enough ideas to occupy the thinking of an average person for a long, long time. But we accept these things without regard to their deeper meanings and so without creative response in personal development. We do not think; we copy. We deal with our ideas as we do with unearned money — "easy come, easy go"; and in place of insight and convictions we have commentaries.

Our selfishness, our willfulness, our superficiality, and our lack of moral courage tend to be expressed in certain types of sinful attitudes which can be distinguished for the sake of analysis, but which merge into each other and influence each other. Any division which we make is an arbitrary one, but the following will perhaps answer our present purpose:

> Sinful attitudes toward God: rebellion, ingratitude, unwillingness to trust him
>
> Sinful attitudes toward the truth: refusal to seek or to accept truth, covering up the truth, hypocrisy and profession without deeds
>
> Sins of conduct or of attitude toward other men: theft, covetousness, hatred, lack of compassion, malicious gossip, unwillingness to forgive

Sins which we share and perpetuate in our corporate
life: low public morality, graft, irresponsibility
toward the underprivileged, militarism
Sins of the flesh: fornication, adultery, overindul-
gence, dissipation of physical gifts

If we study this catalog, we shall see that all of these sins
are violations of the first great commandment: "Thou shalt
love the Lord thy God with all thy heart, and with all thy
soul, and with all thy mind."[2] It is the attempt to avoid the
obligations laid on us by this great commandment which is
at the root of all our sinning.

ATTITUDE TOWARD GOD

Many men, and large sections of society, live in a mood
of indifference toward God. This indifference is hard to justify
under scrutiny. It grows out of an unwillingness to face
searching questions which ought to be faced, such questions
as: "What obligations go with the gifts by which I live?"
The attitude of people who live on the bounty of God and
then act as though all they live by is truly their own is not
unlike that of the man who finds a watch and pockets it without thought or with the explanation that he is not interested
in watchmakers, or on the assumption that the watch just
happened to be there. No man is a *moral* man, in any exalted
sense of that term, who takes the gifts of God without acknowledgment or response.

There are other searching questions which many of us
avoid facing — such as: "What do I do with Jesus and the
prophets?" "How far am I my brother's keeper?" "What
answers shall I give to life's intimations of immortality?" To
pass these questions by as though they are of no moment is
to refuse to take life seriously, and worse. It is to refuse to
take God seriously. Long ago David stated that the fool
hath said in his heart, "There is no God," and then David
went on to explain that the fool he had in mind was not

119

lacking in intelligence, but in morals; this fool had a vested interest in a way of life which ignored God.[3] Modern psychology has made us realize that a vested interest, or a fear, or a reluctance does not have to be present in consciousness to influence thought and action. While this does not justify a hectoring or intolerant attitude toward those who find faith difficult or unacceptable, it does make clear the morally untenable position of those who, whether they believe in God or not, acknowledge no obligations to society except those which society imposes and enforces.

As we have seen, our attitude toward God can be shown in open rebellion or in indifference. It can also be shown in seeming allegiance which is not taken seriously. It is not enough to "confess the Lord Jesus" and to belong to the church. Life asks, "Is your attitude toward God genuine?" We all know that this question has to be asked, for if the first sin is rebellion the second and related sin is hypocrisy.

There are times when it seems even more difficult to change a hypocrite into a genuine disciple than it is to convert an avowed sinner from his rebellion. The hypocrite wears the livery of religion, talks its language, and perhaps even occupies its home; but he neither breathes its spirit nor lives by its laws. Time and time again Jesus commanded his disciples to have faith in God and to "beware . . . of the leaven of the Pharisees, which is hypocrisy."[4] Having enlisted in the service of their Lord it was necessary that they should never mistake the letter of the law for its spirit, the ritual for righteousness, nor the appearance for reality. As one of the most eminent of disciples wrote many years later, "He that doeth righteousness is righteous."[5] He is not righteous who merely wears the uniform.

Many who are not hypocrites nevertheless find it easy to confuse respectability with goodness. All of us share this difficulty in some degree. Like modern Jack Horners, we pull out the plum from the pie of life and say how good

120

we are, when really there is little connection between finding plums and goodness.

> Sin has many aliases and can swiftly shift its guise to gain a welcome into any company. Sin in the slums is gross and terrible. It staggers down the streets, blasphemes with oaths that can be heard, wallows in vice unmentionable by modest lips. Then some day prosperity may visit it. It moves to a finer residence, seeks the suburbs or finds domicile on a college campus. It changes all its clothes. No longer is it indecent and obscene. Its speech is mild, its civility is irreproachable. It gathers a company of friends who minister to pleasure and respectability, and the cry of the world's need dies unheard at its peaceful door. It presses its face continually through the pickets of social allowance, like a bad boy who wishes to trespass on forbidden ground but fears the consequence. Its goodness is superficial seeming; at heart it is as bad as it dares to be. It has completely changed its garments, but it is the same sin—indulgent, selfish, and unclean. Sin, as anyone can easily observe, takes a very high polish.[6]

SINS OF SOCIETY

Not all sin is individual. There are corporate sins which are characteristic of nations and communities and which are echoed in the lives of many of the individuals of these groups. Race prejudice is at once one of the most difficult of these to explain and one of the most difficult to uproot. Materialism, secularism, the hunger for power and status, and such attitudes and appetites form a social atmosphere which strongly influences the individual and which is in turn maintained because the individual responds in kind.

Any adequate history of our times must take note of the exploitation of backward races by more powerful nations, the cult of blind and selfish nationalism, the accepted abandonment of truth in international relations, the debasing of men and women for a profit (alcohol, tobacco, drugs, prostitution), the whole war system, and similar sins of our collective life. These corporate sins are all members of the same family, and

121

support each other and grow strong together. Let us take gambling as an example. The average American who places a two-dollar bet on the World Series may not feel that he is contributing to the spread of evil in our world. Like many of his fellows he may think that a small bet is harmless, a part of our way of life. However, according to a *Life* editorial of June, 1950, about 50,000,000 adult Americans and quite a number of minors gamble. The total they bet each year runs over $30,000,000,000. Six billion of this $30,000,000,000 is profit for the gambling bosses and syndicates of the United States. This amount is more than the combined profits of the hundred largest manufacturing companies in the country. It finances the other enterprises of the underworld bosses. Crime on a large scale is actually paid for by the seemingly "harmless" two-dollar bet.

One of the most powerful facts which protects evil and carries it forward from generation to generation is its profitableness. To quote Dr. Rauschenbusch,

> Ordinarily sin is an act of weakness and sidestepping followed by shame the next day. But when it is the source of prolific income, it is no longer a shamefaced vagabond slinking through the dark, but an army with banners, entrenched and defiant. The bigger the dividends, the stiffer the resistance against anything that would cut them down. When fed with money, sin grows wings and claws. . . . If the love of money is the root of all evil, and if selfishness is the essence of sin, such an expansion of the range and storage capacity of selfishness must necessarily mark a new era in the history of sin, just as the invention of the steam engine marked a new era in the production of wealth. Drink, overeating, sexualism, vanity, and idleness are still reliable standardized sins. But the exponent of gigantic evil on the upper ranges of sin is the love of money and the love of power over men which property connotes.[7]

What a heritage our love of money is causing us to leave for our children! What a different heritage might be theirs if

122

we should be transformed by the renewing of our minds so as to know for ourselves the good and acceptable and perfect will of God.[8]

Not infrequently the stranglehold of sin is strengthened, and its murderous nature hidden, by its association with some desirable attitudes and experiences. Evil is transmitted by being idealized. Alcoholism is associated with good fellowship; war and its kindred evils march in close company with honor and manliness; industrial oppression and economic thievery link arms with laudable ambition and business acumen; graft shelters under the cloak of public service. We shall have exposed drunkenness for what it is when we can show how it shatters friendships and homes and lives; war, when it can be seen in all its horror, betraying and destroying honor and courage; economic dishonesty, when we can show how it lives on the body of the people; and graft, when people see it as a leech fattening on the lifeblood of public affairs.

PERSONAL WRONG

Sin blunts the conscience and blinds us to the reality of what we truly are. It is an amazing fact that outright criminals are the hardest to convince that they have done anything wrong, whereas the greatest spirits of the race are often brokenhearted about what most of us might consider very little things. As a typical example, Scarlet O'Hara in *Gone With the Wind* was stricken with conscience when she first began to open her husband's mail. But after a time she felt no compunctions at all. We have all experienced this in one way or another. This characteristic of sin leads to our awareness of sin in the lives of others, and our blindness to its existence in our own life.

The moral stability of our generation depends on our willingness to face these facts squarely, for the strength of sin lies in those shortcomings for which we excuse ourselves. A traveler in the northern part of Scotland tells us that on one occasion, when he was walking on the moors, he saw a golden eagle rise from the ground and soar with majestic sweep high into the heavens. As he watched, the bird seemed to hesitate for a moment, but then went on again. Then it hesitated still again, but again went on. A third time it hesitated, but this time instead of recovering the bird fell headlong to the earth. The traveler went forward and, finding the bird, turned it over and saw that before leaving the moor the eagle had taken hold of a live weasel. In the course of flight the animal had been drawn close to the bird's body, and there had sucked away its lifeblood. In much the same way, those besetting sins which we hug to ourselves, and for which we find such plausible excuses, drain us of the inner strength which could send us soaring to the heights. The insight of the Psalmist was true to life when he prayed,

> Who can understand his errors? cleanse thou me from secret faults. Keep back thy servant also from presumptuous acts; let them not have dominion over me; then shall I be upright, and I shall be innocent from the great transgression.[9]

Our group sinning is built on our personal shortcomings. We are sentimentalists who can be reached quickly and easily by a hard-luck story or by the necessities of a little child, but we have lost our capacity to sustain these feelings. We forget that the mass of society is composed of individuals, and we are unaware of the results of our actions in the lives of other persons. We divide life into compartments and say that "business is business," and as businessmen we do what we would not approve as religious men. To the sensuality, drunkenness, sullenness, vindictiveness, jealousy, and ill temper of an earlier age we have added a heartlessness and an inhumanity which is only possible in a machine age. We drive hard bargains and live hard lives and adopt for ourselves the slogan, "Every man for himself." Through our political and industrial organizations we commit sins on unseen but

124

real persons which we would not think of committing on people whom we meet face-to-face.

THE WAY OF SALVATION

Your sins and mine are not primarily deliberate acts of self-will, but are links in the great chains of habit. By repeated acts of transgression some of these habits have merged into physical appetites. The sensualist, the drunkard, the liar, the man of habitual ill temper find that when they would do good, evil is present within them.[10] This is true with all of us in regard to our besetting sins. The first step toward our redemption is to recognize our sinfulness, and to face the problem of sin instead of excusing it. The outcry of Paul is born of true insight into the facts of our situation: "Who shall deliver me from the body of this death?"[11] Paul knew that more than a change of heart or a change of mind or a change of will is required to overcome the power of sins which have become entrenched in habit. Only God can do this. But he can.

How God breaks the power of evil habits and evil appetites will be discussed later; but we cannot close this section of our discussion without reaffirming our basic Christian conviction that though sin is a dreadful and an entrenched reality, there is power in the gospel both to turn sinners from their sinning and also to break the power of past evil in the lives of those who give God the place he desires and deserves in their lives.

-----

1. Mark 7:20, 21.
2. Matt. 22:36.
3. Ps. 53:1.
4. Luke 12:1.
5. I John 3:7.
6. Harry Emerson Fosdick, *The Meaning of Faith* (New York: Association Press, 1950), pp. 240, 241.

7. Walter Rauschenbusch, *A Theology for the Social Gospel*, pp. 66, 67.
8. Rom. 12:2.
9. Ps. 19:12, 13.
10. Rom. 7:21.
11. Rom. 7:26.

16 | Agency in the Modern World

W E LIVE IN "the dispensation of the fullness of times" when all past history seems to be coming to culmination. Nevertheless, for those who have eyes to see, the experiences of the modern world confirm the basic affirmations of the Christian order as fully as did the experience of our grandfathers.

We also live in the machine age. Machines which men have built can now do in a few hours things which would have taken a lifetime a few generations ago. Automation has become a major factor in our industrial and social life. But these machines do not bring themselves into being, nor do they operate outside the limits set in their creation by the men who make them. The emergence of the machine age itself testifies to the tremendous significance of free inquiry and experimentation, and emphasizes the moral responsibility of men of understanding. That many front-rank scientists are aware of this became evident when the makers of the A-bomb gave public expression to their disquietude over the uses to which political leaders might put atomic power.

PERSONAL ASPECTS OF LIFE IMPORTANT

When we look carefully at the requirements and implications of this age of science and machinery, we become more and more aware of the importance of the personal aspect of

127

life without which neither science nor invention can exist. It is an age when freedom and responsibility go hand in hand and have tremendous significance beyond the lives of those who might be concerned in any specific project. And it is an age when the kind of intelligence which can build a machine must be applied to the building of life, even though life involves factors which the machine can never encompass. The man who can plan or make the machine may be a sinner in the very fact of refusing to use nobly the intelligence with which he has been endowed and the understanding recently won.

When Sir Francis Bacon came to formulate the spirit of empirical science, as he saw it, he said: "We cannot command Nature except by obeying her." By "obedience" Bacon meant the disciplined, patient, and honest observation and scrupulously truthful reporting which are at the root of the empirical method. This is not easy. To make a technique of seeing the facts truly, without bias or prejudice or self-interest, is one of the immense moral achievements of the race. Thus at the very foundation of science is a profound and active humility: "In order to master, we must first obey." It is not too much to say that this is akin to the requirements of the Christian way of life. In order to live successfully, or even to know what success is, we must discover what life is about and must learn to obey its basic requirements. And if we discover that in order to find our lives we must lose them, then we must face up to this truth and interpret it in terms of both individual and social action, before our specific discoveries can ever minister to the general good.[1]

Knowledge and moral achievement belong together, but each in its own sphere. It is not too much to say that modern men have a specially strong obligation to learn how to act with wisdom and skill and in the spirit of dedication. The needs of our time demand that the church and the university shall work as partners, for the church needs the knowledge which the scientist pursues and the power which the inventor multiplies if it is to make its goodwill effective. On the other hand, the university needs the church for, by itself, the university supplies no sense of purpose, no moral insights, not even the atmosphere of freedom which is finally essential to achievement.

DEPERSONALIZATION IN THE MACHINE AGE

One of the root causes of sin in our day is the depersonalization of industry and of life in general which seems to go hand in hand with the machine age. Men are often called "machinists." The government keeps track of them through a vast and complicated system of numbering. Every man is a statistic, and his life is recorded in terms of his contributions to statistical data. The profitable use of machinery has become a basic factor in the organization of the industry, with far-reaching social and spiritual repercussions. The way out of this does not appear to be through the abandonment of machinery and statistical notation and research, but by recognizing the importance of the individual despite the necessities of mass production and mass enumeration. To use a machine is not sinful, but to use this machine without regard to the human consequences of its use is sinful. Moreover, such disregard of the rightful human factor in the social order is disruptive of that order, the disregard of the human factor in social and industrial life tends to destroy even the ends which it seems to serve. Chairman Clarence Francis of General Foods put it this way:

> You can buy a man's time, you can buy a man's physical presence at a given place; you can even buy a measured number of skilled muscular actions per hour a day. But you cannot buy enthusiasm; you cannot buy initiative; you cannot buy loyalty; you cannot buy the devotion of heart, mind, and soul. You have to earn these things.[2]

In this connection we need to be aware of the remoteness from each other which our age tends to breed. Face-to-face relationships are a great force in keeping conduct on a decent moral level. It is when we do not see our acts in terms of their personal consequences that these acts lack the qualifying element of responsibility which should rightfully accompany them. In 1935 Theodore Quinn, son of a workingman, was selected as vice-president of the huge General Electric Company. There was a good prospect that before very long he would succeed Gerard Swope as president. Yet Theodore Quinn, still in his early forties, soon handed in his resignation. Later he explained, saying: "I began to realize that I was serving no socially worthwhile purpose in helping a giant to become even bigger." Quinn believed that there is a lost element in modern life which he identified as

> living out one's life in the company of people who really know each other, deep down, and who, living in one community, usually face together social discipline, integration, and maturity. The absorption of human lives in industrial centralization, and in the techniques of less responsible mass movements, belittles the individual. The loss of conscience, mutual respect, consideration, and wholesome humanity becomes greater than any possible gain.[3]

A Larger Moral Arena

Undoubtedly, our machine civilization has brought to a larger number of people greater comfort and education and leisure time. We have gone far toward emancipating the worker from the more onerous burdens of his employment. Yet we still need to ask whether these things of themselves have given new meaning to life. Do such things as these provide the strength and purpose to meet the problems which the machine civilization itself imposes?

The late Halford E. Luccock described sin in a premachine age as a solitary horseman waiting at the bend of a dark and lonely road, ready to hold up the first stagecoach to appear. This sin, he said, was stark black against white, an outlaw with a price on his head. Dr. Luccock then went on:

130

But who can recognize, much less apprehend, the modern Dick Turpin? He does not recognize himself. He rides no horse, he carries no gun. He is as gentle as any cooing dove. Yet in thousands of cases he lays a highwayman's tax on every kitchen in the land, on the shops of a thousand industries, using the polite mechanisms of the industrial and political complexities of a power and mass production age. . . . Perhaps it is a monopoly on some natural resources, such as power, steel, iron, or aluminum, which enables some individual or group to gouge hundreds of millions of dollars under the forms of law, from helpless economic vassals. Just as Dick Turpin is said to have shared his plunderings with the poor, so the modern grandees of the Turpin Utilities Company or the Turpin Manufacturing Company, with the generous mood and gesture fling dividends to public enterprises rendering real service, sometimes even to Turpin University or St. Richards Church.

That single contrast, admittedly oversimplified, helps to illustrate the fact that while the basic moral problem is unchanged the moral arena is much larger than it was a few generations ago.

The current decades with their revolutionary concepts concerning the nature of the universe, of time and space, of matter and man, have made necessary new definitions not only of atoms and nebulae, but also of the precise meaning of sin and salvation. It is difficult to emphasize this too strongly. Ever since the close of the Apostolic age Christian people have defined sin very largely in terms of personal maladjustment between the sinner and his contemporaries. We should not underemphasize the very great importance of such maladjustments, but must point out that to find the climax of sin in such a time as this we must not linger over the man who swears, or the woman who gets drunk, or the Saints who disregard the Word of Wisdom. Sin must no longer be seen merely in individual and personal terms. Surely, if there is any gradation among sinners, we must give a prominent place to those who flaunt the love of God for the common man by turning the resources of a nation into the private property of a favored few, or who make a travesty of justice through their selfish application of their peculiar skills.

We cannot go back to an earlier stage of civilization. In fact, it would be unchristian of us to attempt to do so even if we could. Modern life has taught us that the increase of productivity is a precondition to the abolition of poverty, and that the increase of medical knowledge is a precondition of the abolition of pain and disease, and having seen these things, we are under obligation to see that the conditions of progress are met. We must go forward, and not backward. But going forward necessarily involves solving the moral and spiritual problems appropriate to our time. Unless we win on this level all our seeming victories elsewhere are but a sham.

THE PROFIT MOTIVE

Among both religious and business men there has been widespread discussion of a profit motive. In the framework of modern capitalism it would seem that profits are essential, and no adequate substitute has been found. Without profit there is no possibility of building reserves for such things as expansion, experimentation, and wage stabilization. But the lust for profits for their own sake, or as an indication of commercial success, or as a means to power can be a devastating thing. We see this when we realize that a small group of directors sitting in comfort in a conference room far removed from the noise of the machinery which they control can vote an "adjustment to market conditions" which is in truth an adjustment dictated by the profit motive, which may well spell out the difference between starvation and sufficiency for thousands of men and women and children whom they will never see. From the point of view of the average man, and from the point of view of its cumulative effect throughout society, the lust for profit is no less disastrous when it is exhibited by thousands of small businessmen who are determined to "get on" or who feel that imponderable social and economic forces demand their servitude to the prevailing greed for gain.

None of this is intended to imply that if only men believed in God devoutly, giving him the true love of their hearts, the profit motive could be abandoned and its accompanying inequities redressed overnight. What it is intended to indicate is that people who are born into a corrupt economic order are in the same situation as people born into a corrupt humanity. There is no salvation for them in going the way of their fellows without any sense of responsibility for reordering their common life. Salvation is to be won within the social order by taking advantage of the insights which expanding experience gives, without conforming to the limitations which growing depersonalization tends to impose, and — above all — by redirecting social activities of every kind toward the purpose of God in the creation of mankind. Whenever men's basic relationship to God is unsound, none of our human problems can be solved satisfactorily. Any solutions we may work out by ourselves and for ourselves will be superficial and temporary. Every so-called solution will contain within it the seeds of its own collapse.

It should also be pointed out that there is in the foregoing no intention to decry aggressive self-expression so long as it is properly conditioned. The primary instincts of each individual are twofold: one set of instincts inclines a man to seek his own welfare while the other takes satisfaction in the welfare of others. We call them egoism and altruism, self-interest and sympathy or fellow-feeling. If a way of life is to be strong and well balanced, it must enlist in its support both of these sets of primary instincts — the egoistic as well as the altruistic.

Man's innate tendency to seek what his own immediate interests demand is potent. It is the altruistic side of man's nature which needs outside support. But it does not follow that self-interest may not be a moral motive, in some forms and in some measure. In a statement for which he is famous, Rabbi Hillel pointed out: "If I am not for myself, who will be for me? If I am for myself alone, of what use am I?" Many self-interested acts are indispensable to the social good. By seeking his own health, education, and efficiency and by realizing the capacities of his own personality — physical, mental, and spiritual — the individual serves the community, also. The better the units, the better the sum. The better the people of this century, the finer the heritage of the next. But this side of our nature, and the demands of an expanding social order, must be responsibly faced. This problem is basically a moral one. Self-seeking is never justifiable when it is merely self-seeking. It must be accompanied by self-dedication. I must get if I would give, but I must be sure to give if I would be true to myself and my neighbor. To ignore the needs of my neighbor is sin.

OUR COMMON RESPONSIBILITY

Great condemnation for the persistence of the ills which prey on mankind must rest on those talented people who fail to assume the responsibility which goes with every gift and talent. Anyone who so fails is flatly refusing to face the intentions prompting his own creation. The prophet of the latter days put his finger unerringly on the sore spot of our spiritual situation when he said: "Woe unto you rich men, that will not give your substance to the poor, for your riches will canker your souls."[4] But although great opportunity means great responsibility, those with lesser opportunities are not free from condemnation, for the word of inspiration continues:

> Woe unto you poor men, whose hearts are not broken, whose spirits are not contrite, and whose bellies are not satisfied, and whose hands are not stayed from laying hold upon other men's goods, whose eyes are full of greediness, who will not labor with their own hands![5]

It is very easy to vent our moral indignation on the shortcomings of others, but here we are reminded that the spirit which prompts wealthy men to their characteristic sins prompts poor men to sins which are just as deadly even though less spectacular.

It is not just the rich among us, but it is our total social order that must be transformed. Two young children were arguing on the way home from church about which was the last book of the Bible. The boy said to his younger sister, "Carol, I tell you the Bible does not end with James; it ends in Revolutions!" This is more true than the boy understood. The word of God does not end with James or with Tom or Dick or Harry. The only worthy end includes the salvation of men's souls and, as a necessary counterpart, the redemption of the society of men in the kingdom of God.

All of these things help to mark out the pressing aspects of the task which confronts a man who would build his life after the order of the Son of God. He must foreswear the peculiar cult of conformity which as been taken over from secular education, and which has become so popular in recent years. In place of this attractive but cowardly and unprogressive notion of adaptation to environment he must set the Christian ideal of the transformation of environment. His goal must not be an adjusted personality but a frankly unadjusted personality in the sense that Jesus was unadjusted to the sinful forces of his time. And this in turn means that he must be progressively adjusted to a higher order than man can ever bring into being by himself. He must be a pioneer of the kingdom.

---

1. Ably discussed in *What Man Can Make of Man*, William Ernest Hocking, Harper & Brothers, New York and London, p. 26 ff.
2. Quoted in *Ethics in a Business Suit*, p. 92.
3. *Ibid.*, p. 90.
4. D. and C. 56:5 a.
5. D. and C. 56:5 c.

17 The Human Predicament

WE HAVE SEEN that the highest goal for man is the achievement of the divine purpose in his life and in the lives of his fellows. We have also seen that in the pursuit of this goal man is free and responsible, but that he is also burdened by the darker aspects of his heritage from the race and by his seemingly inescapable place among men who have no desire to do the will of God. But while this is so, it is also certain that Truth has powerful allies in the human soul and in the human situation, and beyond them, no matter how ineffective these allies may appear to be at any specific moment. Men are sinners, but they are not just sinners. God does not coerce us, but neither does he leave us entirely alone. In light of these reflections we come now to ask what can and should a responsibly inclined person do to discharge his responsibility faithfully as a man among his fellows?

CONSCIENCE

One answer commonly given to our query is that a man should always "follow his conscience." When properly understood and as far as it goes, this is sound, for "no dictum is more firmly entrenched in Christian morals than this: conscience must always be obeyed."[1] But we need to understand what is properly meant by conscience and what are its limitations.

Thomas Acquinas called conscience "the mind of men passing moral judgments." Yet this widely approved definition appears to be inadequate in that it restricts conscience to the intellectual field, when conscience also has clear emotional significance. The definition is even more inadequate in that it seems to make conscience a purely human matter.

The justly famous commentators Sandlay and Headlam emphasize the more than human element in conscience when they note that in the Corinthian letter conscience is portrayed as "separated from the self and personified as a further witness standing over against it."[2] And from other passages it is clear that the apostle Paul regarded conscience as a monitor which should by right have considerable authority in the life of the individual. He said with some satisfaction that he had "lived in all good conscience before God" and that he "exercised" himself to this end.[3] Perhaps we shall be helped if we think of conscience as the compelling moral awareness which is born of the meeting of the mind and will of man with the Spirit of God.

While conscience has such important functions that Wordsworth could call it the "Stern Daughter of the Voice of God,"[4] conscience must not be equated with the voice of God. Conscience can and does err and mislead. It can hesitate, and can even become so scarred and hardened as to be almost totally ineffective for good.[5]

Conscience has authority but not infallibility. It is deeply rooted in human nature,[6] but is self-centered and varies with the setting in which it is trained, so that it may be good and clear,[7] or weak and vacillating.[8] In addition to these inadequacies, and going beyond them, is the fact that men so frequently refuse to obey the voice of conscience when this voice is most clear and reliable.[9]

The plain truth is that even an erring conscience should be obeyed, but that the agent who does obey an erring conscience is culpable if it is possible that he could have known

137

better. Conscience must not only be obeyed: it must also be educated and enlightened. Thus the wise man wrote, "Keep thy heart with all diligence" by which he meant "Make sure that your conscience is enlightened." This is also what the Psalmist had in mind when he said, "Create in me a clean heart, O God; and renew a right spirit within me."[10] We should do these things, but even then we know that they are not enough. No conscience which is self-centered and socially conditioned, even though well trained and scrupulously followed, is an adequate guide for a man who must face eternity as well as time and who must live with God as well as with his fellows. No man can fulfill the divine purpose in him if his life is merely "the answer of a good conscience" unless God shall do for his conscience something which can be done by no one else.

OBEDIENCE TO LAW

Another answer to our question concerning what a responsible man can and should do to fulfill the purpose of God is that he should keep the law of God. Again, this principle is sound so long as we interpret it rightly and with due regard for its limitations.

The essential idea of those who would fulfill the divine purpose in them by obedience to the commandments of God is that the disorder introduced into life by man's sinful assertion of his own will against the will of God can be overcome, and order be restored, if man will learn to do faithfully what God has commanded him to do. Obviously there is much to commend this point of view, but it does not go far enough. The rich young man who was so concerned about eternal life evidently took some pride in the fact that he had kept the law from his youth up.[11] Even so, he recognized that he still lacked something. From where we now stand we can see that two of these lacks were (1) that he was undoubtedly in error when he said that he had kept *all*

138

these commandments, and (2) having been meticulously careful to keep the law in all its details, he had inevitably taken pride in his self-discipline, and this pride was the father of self-righteousness, which is one of the deadliest of sins and which preys with special appropriateness on those who take seriously their moral responsibility.

A further and fundamental difficulty with the merely legal answer to our query is that legalists tend to construe our relation with God in terms of law, and to regard God as the Chief Magistrate and the Great Bookkeeper. The Pharisees of the time of Jesus listed 613 precepts which must not be infringed. No wonder that even devout Jews thought of life under the law as a bondage,[12] particularly since they were wise enough to know that new forms of sin are constantly appearing and so get ahead of any list of taboos. This is clearly evident in our day, when the advent of the automobile and the moving picture and the wide circulation of obscene literature have given opportunities for sinful conduct which were unknown a few generations ago. We cannot legislate righteousness. The world's ills can never be cured by even the most faithful obedience to the requirements of even the most enlightened legal system. What we need is a new spirit. The answer to men's deepest needs must come from hearts devoted in glad surrender to the will of God.[13]

None of what has been said is intended to present obedience to the commandments of God as unnecessary. Obviously this would be unsound. Nothing but a serious and unreserved acknowledgment of moral obligation can prepare men to play their rightful parts in fulfilling the purpose of God in them. The law written into the nature of man imposes useful disciplines which can become helpful to this end.[14] The law of Moses was a "schoolmaster" to bring the Hebrew people to Christ.[15] It imposed desirable disciplines, but it did not go far enough. Jesus illustrated this when he told his disciples that if the Romans conscripted them to carry baggage for a

139

mile (as Roman law permitted soldiers to do), they should
go a second mile — a mile beyond the requirement of the
law.[16] In certain moods we talk glibly of the "religion of
the second mile." To really fill this we must honor the law
and then go beyond it.

WE CANNOT PAY OUR OWN WAY

A third answer to our query has much in common with
the two we have already considered. It is the answer given
by many religious people and by many others who use their
answer to explain their lack of interest in religion and religious
affairs. Those who give this third answer say that they fulfill
the purpose of God in their creation (or "justify their existence," as they put it) by their good works. These good
works are not quite the same as "the answer of a good conscience," nor are they offered in response to the law of God.
They are what Paul called a man's "own righteousness."[17]

In the Roman letter the apostle Paul is greatly concerned
about man's fulfillment of the divine purpose in his creation
and, most particularly, about the value of the works of
righteousness of a non-Christian man in terms of that man's
answer to the deeper demands of life. As we shall see later,
Paul affirmed that the way of salvation is the way of faith and
not of works. He valued works in their right place as the
partner and evidence of faith; but he saw clearly that no
man can pay his way with his Creator by any work he may
do. How can he when all his strength and skill and resources
come from that same Creator? If he is to pay, he must do
so on terms which the Creator sets — and the Creator never
asks for good works, *except as the expression of love.* Paul
said:

> Though I speak with the tongues of men and of angels,
> and have not charity, I am become as sounding brass, or a
> tinkling cymbal. And though I have the gift of prophecy, and

understand all mysteries, and all knowledge; and though I have all faith, so that I could remove mountains, and have not charity, I am nothing. And though I bestow all my goods to feed the poor, and though I give my body to be burned, and have not charity, it profiteth me nothing.[18]

It is hard for most men to believe this. We find it far easier to persuade ourselves that those who have come to share the finest aspects of the heritage of our race are somehow basically better than others who have achieved no such heights. Dr. H. H. Farmer put it this way:

> How often, as I listen to Bach or Beethoven at a symphony concert, have I caught myself feeling that somehow I was helping human life to be what it was meant to be—really helping things along, far more than the lowbrows who are at the variety show around the corner. And, once again, there *is* truth in this view. There *are* wonderful powers in man. Especially wonderful are his powers of creativeness in art and music and drama; but is it the whole truth—is it, or does it come near, the essential truth? Christianity says emphatically no. And experience also, I think, says no. Hitler, we are told, loved Wagner, and Nero is said to have played the fiddle while Rome burned. I do not doubt that he played it very well.[19]

The finest handiwork of God is not a cultured man. It is a good man among other good men. Culture may well be the handmaid of goodness; but it must not be offered as a substitute. And if we so offer it, God will not accept it.

Actually the works of an ungodly man — ungodly in the sense that he recognizes no responsibility to God — are curiously unbalanced. Such a person may exhibit some of the natural virtues, such as courage or loyalty, in a very high degree; but that same person may, and frequently does, exhibit a surprising lack of the virtue of temperance or of chastity. Then again, he may manifest these virtues strongly under some conditions and hardly at all under other conditions. His courage may be of the physical variety, rather than of the moral order. "The way of man is not in himself; it is not in man that walketh to direct his steps."[20] But "the steps of a good man are ordered by the Lord."[21]

OUR SITUATION

We come, then, to face frankly the fact that of ourselves and by ourselves we can do nothing to guarantee the fulfillment of the divine purpose in us. Without help from above — help such as no man or men can give — the best that we can do is to see a need which we cannot satisfy. Yet to find ourselves even this far on our way is to find ourselves at the gateway of salvation. There is no salvation for men who shut their eyes to the fact of their sins and the sins of their generation. And there is no salvation for those who feel that their only hope is in themselves and in their fellows. But, although we may not have seen it, God has brought us here. And by the grace of God there is fulfillment and peace and joy for those who are willing to learn of the Lord Jesus Christ the divine resources available for the fulfillment of the divine purpose in our creation.

1. Dewar, Lindsay, *A Short Introduction to Moral Theology,* A. R. Mowbray, London, p. 25.
2. Rom. 2:15, ". . . their conscience also bearing witness, and their thoughts the meanwhile accusing or else excusing one another."
3. Acts 23:1, 24:16.
4. "Ode to Duty," *Masterpieces of Religious Verse,* No. 1214.
5. I Tim. 4:2, Titus 1:15.
6. Luke 10:36, Matt. 12:9-12.
7. I Peter 3:16, 21.
8. I Cor. 8:7, 10, 12.
9. Rom. 3:9-20.
10. Ps. 51:10.
11. Matt. 19:20.
12. Gal. 4:5.

13. See Ps. 51, especially verses 10 and 17.
14. Rom. 2:11-15.
15. Gal. 3:24.
16. Matt. 5:41, K.J. or R.S.V. (On consideration, it will be seen that the phrasing of the Inspired Version [5:43], though different, does not point to a basically different interpretation than this.)
17. Rom. 10:1-3.
18. I Cor. 13:1-3.
19. In *God and Men*, Abingdon-Cokesbury Press, New York, p. 75.
20. Jer. 10:23.
21. Ps. 37:23.

Part III

The Way of Redemption

18 Redeeming Love

WE APPROACH this section of our study with certain great convictions. We believe that men are created for a noble purpose. Our lives have an ultimate meaning and destiny known to our Creator and confirmed to us. The purpose of our lives should therefore be his purpose rather than our own. But, endowed with freedom to choose, man has chosen his own way and has turned away from God's love and in toward himself. We have done this so persistently that sin has become part of us both individually and socially. It is in us and in our environment, and goes far to prevent us from fulfilling the purpose of God in our creation.

As we pursue our studies, we need to remember that "sin" is not a word to judge or condemn another. The word "sin" is meaningful only in the context of faith in God. The use of the term points beyond itself to a God who has acted in our behalf. Within the church sin has as its correlate the word "salvation"; they belong together. God does not merely condemn us, but he judges us in order to redeem us.

A few years ago an eager young revivalist was exhorting a captive audience in a soup kitchen on Skid Row. He concluded his remarks by quoting Kipling's poem, "If":

> "If you can talk with crowds and keep your virtue, . . .
> If you can fill the unforgiving minute
> With sixty seconds' worth of distance run . . ."

A voice interrupted from the rear of the room, asking "What if you can't?" This is a profound question. No mere high-powered exhortations to obedience can produce the necessary change in us. It is not a change of mind alone that is required, but a change of the entire personality. Nor is this change an easy thing to accomplish, for it involves abandonment of all that we once were. Sin has become part of us. It has taken hold of us in the form of habits and appetites. We cannot save ourselves. The attempt to do so is like trying to lift ourselves by our own bootstraps. We and our fellows are all caught in the quicksands, and our only hope of salvation lies in someone whose feet are on the firm ground. Our only hope is in God.

God Made Sin His Problem

When our heavenly Father created man he wedded himself to the human race forever, to have and to hold from that day forward, "for better, for worse, for richer, for poorer, in sickness and in health, to love and to cherish" for time and eternity. This is not because of our nature or our works, but because of his nature and purpose. He is that kind of God.

Many years ago the Psalmist sang:

> Make a joyful noise unto the Lord, all ye lands. Serve the Lord with gladness; come before his presence with singing. Know ye that the Lord he is God; it is he that hath made us, and not we ourselves; we are his people, and the sheep of his pasture.[1]

We are the workmanship of his hands and of his heart, too. Because sin blights our lives, and he loves us, he will not turn his back on the problem created by our sinning. Infinite capacity for love means infinite capacity for pain, and so long as God loves us but yet sin reigns in us, the heart of God is broken because of us.[2]

The good news of the gospel is that God has taken the initiative in solving the problem of sin, and that he has solved

147

it. What we could not do for ourselves he has done and is doing for us. We will discuss how God breaks the power of sin at a later point, but let us be sure of this one thing now, that at the heart of the Christian message is the song of victory over sin and death. In this the Christian rejoices with "joy unspeakable."[3] When we turned our backs on God he did not withdraw himself from us and seat himself in some remote place to watch our sin and sorrow and to blame us for destroying his most promising work. Instead he has come all the way with us as though driven by the passion of his love for us.

God wants us infinitely more than we want him. He makes the offering of reconciliation to us, we do not make it to him. It is man who must be induced to accept the divine mercy, and not God who must be persuaded to offer it. The whole of the New Testament rings with this key thought. Its writers make no suggestion that we have to reconcile God to ourselves. Our Father is not holding himself aloof because he is spiteful or angry with us. "God is in Christ, reconciling the world. . . . Be ye reconciled to God."[4] "We love him, because he first loved us."[5] It is his unfailing love that finally "constraineth us" to make his purpose for us our purpose for ourselves.[6]

THE SON OF GOD CONFRONTS MAN'S SIN

In the conflict with sin the chief weapon used by our heavenly Father has been his patient love. Because of this great love he sent his Son to save the world.[7] And because the Lord Jesus loved mankind he came to live among us and to show us in his own life and death what the love of God really means.[8]

The conflict of Jesus with sin is evident at every point in his ministry. When the Master sought out his cousin, John, at the very beginning of his work, the Baptist hailed him, "Behold the Lamb of God, who taketh away the sin of the world."[9] When his work was completed, the Master told his

148

disciples that his blood was to be shed "for the remission of their sins."[10] Still later, when about to bid farewell to the men who were to carry his message to the world, he "opened . . . their understanding, that they might understand the scriptures, and said unto them, Thus it is written, and thus it behooved Christ to suffer, and to rise from the dead the third day; and that repentance and the remission of sins should be preached in his name among all nations, beginning from Jerusalem, and ye are witnesses of these things."[11]

The life and ministry of the Lord Jesus Christ were all of one piece. It is unsound to say that any part of his life or death is more significant for our redemption from sin than any other part. He is our perfect example of how life should be lived. He is also our perfect example of how death should be faced. But, beyond these things, he is the author and guarantor of our salvation because of what he is in time and in eternity. Before Jesus came no one ever had any idea of the infinite dimensions of the love of God. But to the degree that we have come to know the love of God in Christ Jesus we also know that this love did not begin with the coming of Christ to earth, nor did it end with his ascension into heaven. This love was manifested in creation, and is constantly manifested in judgment[12] and in intercession,[13] and will be manifested in glory.[14]

To know Jesus is to know that God is love, and that love is from eternity to eternity. Looking backward we are assured that there was no need for men to rebel against God in order to enter into life, and, looking forward, we know that we do not need to continue in rebellion in order to be men. If we love and trust God as the disciples nearest the Master came to love and trust the Lord Jesus, we shall win the victory over sin as his disciples, the glad captives of his love.

THE SPIRIT AND THE VICTORY

The Son of God revealed the splendor of the love of God, but only through the ministry of the Spirit of God. God must make himself known both within and without before we can come to understanding. Capacity to recognize greatness depends on the presence of the greatness which is to be seen, and also on the ability to sense what is there to see.

The primary task of Jesus is to reveal God to man. This revelation is, in a sense, objective. The primary task of the Holy Spirit also is to reveal God to man. But the revelation of the Holy Spirit is subjective. Just as God seeks after us in the life and ministry of his Son, so also he seeks after us in the persuasive inner ministry of his Holy Spirit which teaches and warns and strengthens and reminds and guides. The Holy Spirit is God at work from within. Moreover, just as the incarnation of the Son of God indicates how truly God and man can be knit together, so that no one can draw a clear line of distinction between Divinity and humanity, so also the indwelling of the Holy Spirit in the inner life of a man is such that no one can say what inner propulsion is divine and what is human. This does not mean that the personality of the man of God is stultified, but that it is enriched. It is the peculiar mission of the Spirit of God, which is Love, to promote both the freedom and the discipleship of the believer.

The spirit which enlightened the disciples when Jesus was on earth, so that they knew him to be the Messiah,[15] and which was evident at Pentecost and on numerous other occasions of endowment, always bore witness of Christ in the sense of making meaningful the life and teachings of the Master. It is the Spirit of Love and Light, and without it there is no sound perception of the divine purpose which God set forth in its fullness in the life of Jesus nor of the purpose which he seeks to fulfill in the lives of men. Nevertheless, enlightenment is not for every man. It is only for those who can be persuaded to do their part. There was no witness of the Spirit for the opinionated Pharisees, nor for the money-loving Felix,[16] nor yet for the power-seeking Simon.[17] But it was available to the Philippian jailer,[18] and to the Ephesian disciples,[19] and even to the gentile Cornelius.[20]

We are redeemed by the love of God, and as we substitute love for selfishness as the ruling passion of our lives. The apostle Paul put it this way:

> If any man live in Christ, he is a new creature; old things are passed away; behold, all things are become new, and receiveth all the things of God, who hath reconciled us to himself by Jesus Christ, and hath given to us the ministry of reconciliation: to wit, that God is in Christ, reconciling the world unto himself, not imputing their trespasses unto them; and hath committed unto us the word of reconciliation. Now then we are ambassadors for Christ, as though God did beseech you by us; we pray you in Christ's stead, be ye reconciled to God.[21]

In another letter to the Corinthian saints Paul made the preeminence of love even more clear. He had been giving counsel concerning the exercise in public of various kinds of spiritual gifts. He then interjected what is perhaps his most famous passage, the hymn to charity, before again picking up the main line of his argument:

> Though I speak with the tongues of men and of angels, and have not charity, I am become as sounding brass, or a tinkling cymbal. And though I have the gift of prophecy, and understand all mysteries, and all knowledge; and though I have all faith, so that I could remove mountains, and have not charity, I am nothing. And though I bestow all my goods to feed the poor, and though I give my body to be burned, and have not charity, it profiteth me nothing.[22]

Our task as we seek to fulfill the purpose of God in us is to share the load which God carries because of his love. It is to sit down by the suffering and take their burdens on our hearts; to get under the weight of the world's sin until we feel the shame and the guilt of it as though it were all our own; to seek out the root causes of the evils preying on humanity, and to dedicate our lives to fighting these evils. It is only as we do these things in love that we ourselves get into

151

the way of life. Then the whole attack on the problem of sin is changed, both within us and around us. We no longer give primary concern to the bookkeeping of salvation, or to the piling up of "merits." Our only concern is that we shall act as becomes the children of the God of love:

> O Cross, that liftest up my head,
> I dare not ask to fly from Thee;
> I lay in dust life's glory dead,
> And from the ground there blossoms red
> Life that shall endless be.[23]

1. Ps. 100:1-3.
2. D. and C. 36:6-9.
3. I Pet. 1: 8, 9.
4. II Cor. 5:19, 20.
5. I John 4:19.
6. II Cor. 5:14.
7. John 12:47.
8. John 1:14.
9. John 1:29.
10. Matt. 26:24.
11. Luke 24: 44-47.
12. I Pet. 4:5, Acts 10:42, and others. He "is ready to judge the quick" as well as "the dead." Judgment is a present fact as well as a coming event.
13. Heb. 7:24.
14. Matt. 24:34, D. and C. 76:5, 7 ff.
15. Matt. 16:18.
16. Acts 24:22-27.
17. Acts 8:18-21.
18. Acts 16:29-33.
19. Acts 19:1-6.
20. Acts 10:44-47.
21. II Cor. 5:17-20.
22. I Cor. 13:1-3.
23. George Matheson, *Masterpieces of Religious Verse*, No. 720.

19 | Creative Forgiveness

THE CHRISTIAN solution for the problem of sin centers in *forgiveness*. This at once puts both the problem and the solution on a personal plane, for "forgiveness" is an intensely personal word. It has to do with persons and personal relationships. In using this word in this connection we are saying that the problem of sin is not primarily a legal matter, nor an educational matter, nor yet a sociological matter; it is fundamentally a personal matter. Although education, better housing, and improved hospitalization are all helpful in their places, they do not touch the blindness and rebellion which are at the heart of sin. Only an enlightening and renewing experience with God can do this. Forgiveness is such an experience. Other adjustments are important, but they are secondary. They follow after.

Sin has separated us from God and has driven us from our Father's home into a far country. This far country of sin is not suited to our nature. We are unhealthy and unhappy so long as we stay there. Lacking a sense of companionship with God, we are lonely and forsaken. But when our sins are forgiven we are welcomed back home again and recognized as sons and heirs. Barriers that might make us afraid to face our Father are put behind us. Once more we can attack the tasks of life with peace and joy in our hearts and with the consciousness of our Father's loving care in every time of difficulty.

This word forgiveness is one of the most significant words in the vocabulary of the disciple of Jesus, and we must beware of degrading it. Forgiveness is not the same as canceling a debt, for in the long run easy cancellation of the debt of sin would make us think too lightly of our sinning. Again, forgiveness does not mean the overlooking of sin. To overlook sin as if it hardly mattered is not the nature of divine forgiveness. Sin matters greatly with God; in fact, he alone fully understands the tragic consequences of sin. This divine perception of the horror of sin is what makes the fact of our Father's forgiveness so glorious.

The heart of forgiveness lies in the overcoming of sin by the power of love. When a sinner is forgiven, right relations are restored between him and God. The more love enters into the situation the more meaningful forgiveness becomes. If a man trades at my store and then fails to pay his bill, I may write off the debt as a matter of business expediency; but the man is not truly forgiven until I feel kindly toward him in spite of my loss and our personal relationship is again what it was before. This is quite difficult to do; but when the personal element enters, forgiveness is even more difficult. If this man should come into my home and rob me of the affections of my wife it may be that I could do nothing about his sin against me, but just passing a sin over because I cannot do anything is not forgiveness. This man is not forgiven until I have the same attitude toward him that I had before his transgressions. Forgiveness on this plane is infinitely more difficult than it was when nothing was involved but a grocery bill. Indeed, it is impossible until two things shall happen: the love of God must possess my soul, and the sinner must change his attitude toward his sin.

When God forgives our sins he does so because of his great love for us. But that is not all. To readmit us into intimate personal relations with himself without any change in our attitude of sinful rebellion might only confirm us in our sinning. He does not do this; indeed, he cannot. Fellowship is not a one-sided affair, and if our Father is to forgive us and take us back into affectionate relationship with himself, we must be able to share this fellowship. Our sins cannot cease to divide us until we regard them in the same light and take the same attitude toward their elimination.

No good mother can forgive the transgressions of her children lightly. If she did the children would come to regard these transgressions lightly, too. A sinful child must abandon his attitude of rebellion if he is to be truly forgiven and the relationship fully restored. This is not to say that the mother ceases loving the child when he sins, but that forgiveness demands a changed attitude on his part. In the deepest sense it involves recovery of a sense of mutuality. The effort to induce the child to change his ways is often a costly one to both mother and child; nevertheless the significant thing about transgressions in a happy and affectionate family is that love covers this cost. Although there may be hardness of the heart and resentment for a moment, the children know that once they recapture the spirit of mutual affection and common purpose they will find themselves back in the family circle. Once their attitude is changed they will walk once more in the way of love. Forgiveness is this welcoming back of a child who lost the family spirit but who "came to himself"[1] and turned again home.

GOD TAKES THE INITIATIVE

As the sin against love is, by its nature, the worst kind of sin, so forgiveness on this plane is only possible when it is met by love that is full and overflowing. Jesus taught this, and his amazed disciples were captured by his teaching and echoed it again and again. The forgiveness which God offers to men is free, without money and without price so far as he is concerned. Indeed, it has to be. To expect men to make reparation for all the many ways in which they have flouted the love of God is to lay upon them a heavier burden than they can bear. To make forgiveness a subject of bargaining, in which debit and credit amounts are nicely balanced against each other, is to destroy completely the Father-son relationship which Jesus proclaimed. But when we realize that we are all sons of God, even though we have gone off into far countries, we know that nothing can separate us from the love that made and would redeem us. At the least sign of penitence on our part, of the forgivableness which makes forgiveness moral, this love reaches out to us and is found to be sufficient for all our needs.

Our heavenly Father cannot compromise with our sins, but he can and does surround us with inducements to cease our rebellion and to return to him. What a lesson it is to our own narrowness and our own unforgiving spirit to let our thoughts review the company of those whom Jesus loved and served: the centurion, representative of the race that had enslaved his people; a Canaanitish woman, scorned as a heathen; Judas, who was waiting to betray him; the woman of the streets; Peter, who denied him in the hour of his greatest need; and at the last the city that rejected him and the soldiers whose hands drove the nails. Words are like vessels; it is what fills them that counts. Men had talked of love before, but they had to wait until Jesus came to know the full meaning of the word.[2]

If we could only read the New Testament with open eyes, or listen to it as someone would tell the story anew, we might catch once again the wonder of those who first saw Christianity at work in the world. Jesus and his followers knew no hopeless cases. Read the account of Zacchaeus, the publican, who had sold his self-respect for money. Jesus went home with him, made a friend of him, and by the wonder of his friendship shamed the man into a new life.

Think of the story of the woman "taken in adultery." Others jibed at her and would have stoned her, but Jesus restored her self-respect and made her at home in the heart of his company and in the hearts of all those who came to know her story. The book of Acts and the letters written by Paul and John carry on the same story of unfailing triumph. The early Christians knew that it is impossible to overestimate the danger, the shame and the awfulness of sin; but they also knew from experience that "where sin abounded, grace did much more abound."[3]

A NEW HEART

Although the divine forgiveness approaches infinity, there is a place where our heavenly Father draws a sharp line. "If you do not forgive," says the Master, "neither will your Father who is in heaven forgive your trespasses."[4] Our prayer for forgiveness of our trespasses is not complete until we have added to it, in all sincerity of purpose, the qualifying phrase, "as we forgive those who trespass against us."[5] This is not a limit on the willingness of God to forgive, but is only an indication of what true forgiveness is. There is no real forgiveness until the Spirit of God, which leads him to forgive us, finds place in our own hearts and causes us to forgive our fellows. This is the fulfillment of the promise to the prophets of old—"A new heart also will I give you, and a new spirit will I put within you."[6]

The man who continues to hold an unforgiving spirit may ask God to overlook his sins, but what he really wants is not forgiveness but forgetfulness. He is seeking escape from the consequences of sin rather than from sin itself. Forgiveness in the fullest sense is impossible for him until he can receive of the heart and spirit of the new covenant and enter into a new relationship with God and his fellowman.

There is nothing more wonderful in human life than real forgiveness, compassion, and love for other people which

157

puts no barriers in the way once they are willing to abide by the conditions of fellowship. There is a great deal which travels under the name of forgiveness, but which is merely a matter of the lips or which smacks of the bargain counter. But there is no bargaining in the Spirit of Jesus. In the divine forgiveness which our heavenly Father expects us to extend to those who have injured us, love plays the major role. Love overcomes the hatred, the resentment, and the hurt which we feel when we have been unjustly treated. Love provokes in us an eager desire that he who has sinned against us may be changed in heart so that a complete restoration may be accomplished and the old fellowship restored. Once this miracle takes place, the one who has been forgiven must be base indeed if he will again betray the trust placed in him. Such forgiveness, much more than punishment, will hold the willing and affectionate cooperation of those who were once selfish and resentful.

THE FUTURE DECIDES

There is a sense in which it is true that what is past is beyond recall. No one can turn back the hands of the clock and erase or change that which has already happened. The years which the drunkard has dissipated are gone, and the stain of his wasted opportunity is dark in his heart and mind. But there yet remains a sense in which all this can be changed. The drunkard can continue to dissipate his strength, to squander his resources, to impoverish his family, and to flout the will and purpose of God. Or, on the other hand, he can enter into the new relation with God which we have called forgiveness, changing his own attitude to meet the offer of friendship and pardon which comes from God. When he does this the past is no longer with him as something to be excused and justified, but as something to be hated and overcome. It stays as an example of what his life was without God, and as an evidence of the power of God to save him from sin.

So with other transgressions. They too can be changed. The future has yet to decide what past sin shall mean. Later experience may impart a new and beautiful meaning to what formerly seemed to be unrelieved disaster—just as a musical chord is affected by other sounds which follow and blend with it, or as a dreary stretch of land along the highway may precede surpassingly beautiful country and so accent one's appreciation of it. This is not just theorizing. It is a fact of experience that men who follow after Jesus constantly find within themselves the power to so deal with past events as to change their significance through the radiance of divine love. In the words of an inspiring writer in this field, "It is not sinning that ruins men, but sinning and not repenting."[7]

Another immediate effect of the restoration of right relations between God and man is that true forgiveness removes at once the sense of guilt and of estrangement from God. Sin always brings with it a certain hardness, as if the soul has become calloused in the struggle of living. The unrepentant sinner is resentful of any attempts to bring him back, and regards such attempts as interference with his personal rights. But when it dawns on him that God is his friend, and that the only barriers to complete communion with divinity are the barriers which he himself has raised, hardness and resentment give way to joyous discipleship. Much of the problem of sin remains, but instead of refusing the help of the Father the one-time sinner now welcomes it.

Because of his respect for us as persons our heavenly Father will not force us to do anything. He will surround us with temptations upward, but he will not force us to take the upward way. He will persuade us, but when we change our way of living we must do so of our own volition. He will forgive us whenever he can persuade us to cooperate in the experience of forgiveness, and when he does we are changed men and women. The scars left by sin may still be visible,

159

but they speak no longer of the death that once threatened us; they speak instead of the life which now is.

---

1. Luke 15:17.
2. Charles Foster Kent, *The Teachings of Jesus* (New York: Charles Scribner's Sons)
3. Rom. 5:20.
4. Mark 11:28.
5. Matt. 6:10-15.
6. Ezek. 36:26, see also Jer. 31:33.
7. H. R. McIntosh, *The Christian Experience of Forgiveness* (New York: Harper and Brothers).

20 The Divine Element in Forgiveness

Since God loves us, and since the essence of forgiveness is the restoration of right relations between God and man, the problem of forgiveness is to make sinful man willing to do his part toward this restoration. Without reconciliation an awful chasm yawns between God and man, so that the divine purpose in us is never seen clearly or understood fully. How is this chasm to be bridged? How shall we learn to look at sin as God looks at it, and to act toward it as God would have us act?

The heart of the Christian message is that God has made the original movement to bridge the chasm between us from the divine side. What we cannot do for ourselves he has done for us. He has reached across the depths, taking on himself the sacrifice and much of the cost, to show us that the only obstacle to peace and reconciliation is in us. In spite of the fact that the transgressions have all been on our side, he has given his Only Son to persuade us to return to his family circle where we belong. "Herein is love, not that we loved God [that is readily understandable], but that he loved us" (in spite of our agelong rebellion).[1] Nothing could ever restore right relations between him and us except the fact that God, who had been wounded by our transgressions, comes all the way to meet us as though he had been the transgressor.

161

All true forgiveness shows sin in a light which was not there before. There is no such thing as casual forgiveness. Genuine forgiveness requires clear thought and deep personal involvement. That is what makes true forgiveness such a searching experience. When a boy sins against his father and against the spirit and standards of his father's home, the father's concern cannot be adequately expressed by merely "preaching" at his son. If there is to be any restoration of the family relations the boy must come to see that his sin wounds his father, and that his father's pain will continue as long as love continues on the one side and sin on the other. And, out of his own love for his father, the son must learn that the wounding of his father is an element in all his sinning. He cannot sin and avoid this result. And there is no way in which the father can ease his own wounds by ignoring the facts of the situation, there is no way in which he can forgive a blind and unrepentant son. Somehow, for forgiveness to be real and creative, the son must be brought to his true self, so that he will stand with his father in sincere repudiation and condemnation of his sinful self.

What if the boy offers easy and shallow excuses? What if he says that his father has taken this thing too seriously, and thereby invites his father to take his own low view of what has happened? If this takes place, and the father agrees by his acts that the son's position is permissible or even sound, he thereby abandons his own high sense of what is right, lets go the one thing which is most likely to clarify his son's moral perception, and clouds the issue for other members of the family who are looking on. No! The only forgiveness that is worth talking about is one in which the father takes the initiative in establishing a new relationship where the son senses his father's love and the burden which sin imposes on his father because of that love. When this is done there is a chance that, out of the son's responsive love, they will be

162

able to stand together in repudiation of what the son has done and of the selfish willfulness which caused him to do it.

OUR SIN AND GOD'S LOVE

As we think about forgiveness it becomes more and more apparent that the possibility of true forgiveness, in the sense of the achievement of right relations, depends on the love and wisdom available for the task. This is true in the family, in society, in the family of nations, and in the family of God.

Human love is the most outgoing experience that men know. It does much to identify the lover with the beloved and to cause each to seek the good of the other, sometimes at great personal sacrifice. But even the most sacrificial human love tends to reach its limits sooner or later. Mothers who would die for the sake of their children cannot control their own tempers when their children are fractious. Husbands who would as willingly die for their families will not take time from their business concerns to walk with them in the difficult paths of childhood and adolescence. Patriots who have shown their willingness to die for their country prove quite unwilling to live for their country and the ideals they once fought for. Among us, what we call "love" is largely a give-and-take affair. The millions of once-promising marriages which are shipwrecked after a few years bears irrefutable testimony to this.

The more inclusive the relationships involved, the greater the demand for loving wisdom. And when we consider the relation between God and man—a relationship which has to do with both time and eternity—love and wisdom beyond what man can supply is quite evidently in demand. Indeed, the love which a man has known as a man among his fellows is such a faint echo of the love which the situation requires that man can make no progress toward reconciliation until God, in his love, reaches out after him and teaches him what true love is. Only when this happens do God and man talk the same language.

163

Throughout his ministry the Lord Jesus Christ was concerned to state and to illustrate the unique characteristics of what his disciples were later to call "love unfeigned."[2] This is pure love, freely given, without regard to reward or reciprocation, concerned only about the good of the loved ones. The Lord found the people "slow of heart to believe." As each new requirement of this love was made clear, more of them hardened their hearts against him and refused to follow him in the way where he sought to lead them.

The clearer Jesus made the obligations of righteousness, the more the Jews hated him. This hatred grew until at the end there was no length of resentment to which his countrymen would not go, no magnaminity which they would not abuse, no treachery that they would not employ. This is the characteristic reaction of unrepentant sin to unswerving love. It can only be overcome by the Spirit of God persuading man from within. Jesus could have answered the hatred which met his own goodness by adopting an attitude of resentment, but to do this would have been to use the coin which men have used all down the generations, and which had led from hatred to still more hatred. Instead, Jesus chose to let the Jews and all the world see in his own person what sin does to innocent men and women. If he had resisted them in their own way, the Jews would have killed him and forgotten him. But they could not forget one who died as Jesus died.

Calvary gave mankind the greatest revelation in history of the awfulness of sin and of the power of forgiving love. Here Jesus showed that real love is not a give-and-take affair, and for that very reason it is stronger than men had ever known that love can be.

CALVARY

What happened to Jesus at Calvary was no accidental development. "This thing was not done in a corner."[3] The crucifixion was not a tragic miscalculation but was "according to the definite plan and foreknowledge of God."[4] Jesus went up to Jerusalem to carry on and to consummate his work. His message had been delivered in the preached word and in the demonstration of power, but he had not yet made dramatically clear the fact that God is in agony for the redemption of mankind. So he took the situation into his own hands, chose the time and place, and set his face steadfastly to go toward Jerusalem. There, in his sermons and in his silences, in his work and in what he failed to do, he was at every point preparing to reveal sin in its true light. His enemies caused his death, but they did not gain their end. It was not an execution but a sacrifice. The cross carries the meaning which Jesus gave it—it speaks his message, not the message of his enemies.

Those who actually participated in the crucifixion of Jesus had no clear knowledge of all that they were doing. Yet when they got away from their task and looked back on it they could not feel easy about what they had done. Neither those who shared in the sacrifice, nor the many others who had cried out, "Release unto us Barabbas"—nor any of us who have looked at Jesus across the centuries—can ever feel easy about him as he hangs there. It is as though Jesus says to all of us, "I want you to see sin as it really is; not when you are hot with passion, nor when your fear for your property rights has blinded you to the truth, but in its final consequences. You can see in me—here on the cross—the picture of what sin really does and the length to which God will go to have you understand. If this double revelation will not move your heart to repentance, nothing will. I die gladly in the hope that my cruel death will cause you to hate any sin which separates you from the love of God."

Insofar as deep consciousness of the meaning of sin is the first step toward salvation from sin, the cross of Christ has been the most effective instrument of redemption that men have ever known. Not even the life of the Lord Jesus has quickened men to such horror of sin as his death has done.

Nor is the cross the end of the story. The mother who loves her reprobate son does not look forward to any release from her suffering for him except the release that comes with his reformation. Until he is made over again, there is no peace for her anywhere. If she could have her choice, she would purchase the power to persuade him toward righteousness at any cost to herself. This is but a faint illustration of how our heavenly Father has felt toward his wandering and rebellious children from the beginning of time. His suffering love is not an isolated event, nor is it an eddy in the main current of history. What God did in Christ on the cross, God is always doing. On Calvary Jesus showed us in the agony of one great hour how God has felt and what God has done right down the ages.[5] There is no release for him so long as our sin continues. "If to bear our sins means to go where the sinner is, and refuse either to leave him or to compromise with him; to love a shameful being, and therefore to be pierced by his shame; to devote one's self utterly to his recovery, and follow him with ceaseless ministries, knowing that he cannot be recovered without his consent, and that his consent may be indefinitely withheld—if this is to bear sin, then this is what Jesus did upon the cross and it is the innermost secret of the heart of God."[6]

LOVE DOWN THE AGES

Have you ever tried to defend the character of God before a large audience of scoffers? If you have, you know that some will always mention such "acts of God" as the San Francisco earthquake and fire, the slums of a large city, the widespread starvation in India and China, or the horror of modern warfare. It is impossible for an honest man to refuse to face these facts, for they do constitute a challenge to our belief in a God of love. Except for the cross of Christ

166

we would have no answer for them. Even in the light shed from the cross we do not fully understand. But at least we know that God is not standing aloof from our most deeply entrenched enemy. He is attacking the problem of sin with us. He who gave his Son to bear the load of sin shares with us every other problem that we meet in life, and if we fight sin we fight shoulder to shoulder with God.

If we believe, as we do believe, that on the black day at Calvary the Son of God died for our sake and the sake of mankind, then we must walk with him long enough to catch the message which he gives us from the cross. This message is one of forgiveness and love. We shall never really enter into "the fellowship of his sufferings,"[7] until we pattern our lives after his. His method must be our method also. At one turning point in Jesus' ministry when Satan tried to persuade him to choose another way than that of the cross, the Master told him, "Get thee behind me, Satan; . . . for thou savorest not the things that be of God, but those that be of men."[8] He himself has laid down the supreme law of discipleship: "If any man will come after me, let him deny himself, and take up his cross and follow me."[9]

In the cross of Christ we see the battle against sin at its climax. Without him we are handicapped from the beginning; our pride, our love of gain, and our desire for ease are hostages held by the enemy. So long as these are more dear to us than they ought to be, sin wins. But our Lord has given himself as a ransom. No one who has known the love manifested at Calvary can ever again think too highly of himself, his possessions, or his ease. And once these things are valued for their actual worth, but no more, sin has lost its major hold on us. We are henceforth free as we have never been free before.

---

1. I John 4:10.
2. II Cor. 6:6; I Peter 1:22.

3. Acts 26:26.
4. Acts 2:23, R.S.V.
5. D. and C. 36:6-11 ff.
6. W. R. Maltby, *The Meaning of the Cross,* The Epworth Press.
7. Phil. 3:10.
8. Matt. 16:24.
9. Matt. 16:25.

21 | Faith and Forgiveness

WE HAVE ENDEAVORED to look at life squarely, without thinking of ourselves more highly than we ought to do, and have given particular attention to the barriers raised by our personal iniquities and our social transgressions against the fulfillment of the divine purpose in us. We have also considered the cross of Christ as the epitome of the divine attempt to bridge the chasm which our sinning has created between us and God. We now ask again, "In view of the seriousness of sin and its place in our personal and social life, what can we do in order to enter into right relations with God? What can we do to answer the purpose of our creation, both individually and socially?"

Our task is not just to overcome specific sins. The problem is not with *sins,* but with *sin.* We must abandon all demands for our own self-centered way, and quit our rebellion against God. We must have a change of heart and mind, and start to live anew; specific changes will grow out of this basic readjustment.

FAITH AS TRUST

The first thing that God requires of us — and this requirement is written into the very nature of the situation — is that we shall have faith in him. We are lost, far from the

169

main highway of life. We must trust someone to lead us back. He asks us to trust him.

In the early years of the seventeenth century, the Earl of Strafford was loyal to Charles I of England during the king's difficulties with Parliament. In the service of Charles, Strafford incurred the hatred of the Commoners, but Charles said: "I am the king. I will stand by you. Without my signature you cannot be hurt." For a time the king was not hard pressed, and Strafford was safe; but when the fortunes of war turned against the king the Earl was arrested by the Parliamentary officers, tried for treason, found guilty, and sentenced to death. Remembering the king's promise, Strafford was not unduly dismayed. But Cromwell and the other Parliamentary leaders were determined to have the Earl's life. They maneuvered Charles into a difficult situation and under this pressure the king signed the death warrant. It is small wonder that when Strafford heard the news he echoed the words of David, "Put not your trust in princes, nor in the son of man, in whom there is no help."[1]

From the cross where he gave his life for us Jesus says, "Why not trust me? Why not trust my Father?" When we put our trust in God we are taking no such risks as Strafford took. The fact that it is the Lord whom we worship and seek to serve puts our trust on an entirely different basis. Ultimately, it is only faith in the unfailing God that endures and prevails.

Faith in God is not just a matter of intellectual assent to facts about God or about Jesus. It is a movement of the heart toward him in confident trust in which we recognize our own need (someone has called it our "lostness") and accept his way out because we love him and believe in him. Such trust in God does not answer all our questions. Indeed, it is not necessary that it should. What we need in a crisis is not to know all the answers, but to have confidence in someone who does know, and who will lead us toward the light

170

as quickly as we are able to face it. In the nature of things we must "walk by faith, not by sight."[2] Because He knows that this is the only hope for us, and that only in this way can we fulfill the purpose of our creation, our heavenly Father sent his Son into the world to lead us back to him. Jesus came all the way to where we are. Since the chasm created by our sinning was too deep for us to cross, he bridged it from the divine side. Now he pleads with us to cross back over the bridge with him. Unless we are willing to respond to the sacrifice of Calvary with the confident trust which we call faith, that sacrifice is wasted and we are lost.

FAITH AS COMMITMENT OF SELF

The greatest expression of atheism today is not an intellectual rejection of belief in the existence of God, but an unwillingness to commit our lives to God's purpose. There is a lack of faith, so widespread and so characterized by life conducted as if God did not matter, that our society has been labeled "post-Christian."

Faith in God, which is the initial step in restoring right relations between us and our Creator, is not and cannot be a merely passive thing. Faith is not a mere belief that God exists, but a commitment of one's self to God and his ways. Faith is not a substitute for the truth; it is a way of approaching the truth. Nor is faith simple receptiveness. Faith is not mere acceptance; it is self-commitment. It gives itself as well as receiving Christ. In a valid marriage each party pledges the future in permanent self-surrender. Each commits himself to the other in confidence that their future, with all its new revelations of character, will progressively justify an adventure which was launched on the basis of affectionate insight. When we have faith in God we commit ourselves in similar surrender to his way of living. It is as if we build a firm stairway from where we are now to the heavenly country whose radiant glory we cannot yet see. To Jesus, the supremely courageous adventure of the spirit is this adventure of faith. By such faith we build our lives toward God in the confident trust that he will support us as may be necessary at each point of the ascent.

Faith is a declaration of dependence and a vow of allegiance, a surrender of the soul to its rightful King. Consequently, faith in God involves acceptance of his point of view regarding our lives, individually and collectively. It means glad acknowledgment that the life manifest in Christ is the true life of man, and that we were created in order that we might share this life. His life is the visible manifestation of the glory of human nature, the idea itself as well as the concrete prophecy of its moral and spiritual excellence. In the life of Jesus we see the true relation of humanity to divinity, the perfection toward which God designs that we shall be forever approaching. In just the same way the kingdom of God is the idea and the revelation of the divine purpose for society, and the goal to which we ought to move collectively. Our individual and collective goals are inextricably related. It is the very nature of the Christlike person to express his life in kingdom relationships.

Faith in God leads us to confess that his thoughts about our sins are truer than our own thoughts, and that his horror of sin is more fully justified than our own complacency with sin. What God and Christ feel about our wickedness is just and true, and if we truly trust God then we will act toward our sinning as the Father and the Son act toward it. We will share their hatred of it and fight it with every power that God shall give us.

When we are at enmity with God, choosing our way rather than his and refusing to surrender our life to his guidance, we continue to be alienated from him. Our lives remain devoid of the power which comes from communion with him. But when we sincerely and earnestly seek to do the will of God, and give it first place in our lives because we trust him more than we trust ourselves, our lives are filled with power. Now we can enjoy the sense of his presence as we never did before.

In the time of Jesus there was a group of converts to Judaism known as "Proselytes of the Gate" because they contented themselves with sitting in the gate, as it were, without going into the Holy City. If our lives lack the complete abandon of devotion, we become such people. The Father may do much for us, but he cannot take possession of our lives. "Proselytes of Righteousness," on the other hand, were converts who joined themselves wholly to the people of God. They included in their number some truly great men, who were filled with the love of God and represented him in spirit and in truth. It is to such an exalted destiny that we are called.

The faith that we are discussing is a whole-souled and permanent commitment. The important thing is not emotion alone, but devotion. No temporary faith will suffice. A spasmodic faith may win us certain advantages, such as a physical blessing, but faith to be healed of physical infirmity is by no means the highest form of faith. It may even be dangerous instead of being helpful, if it does not lead to complete surrender of the soul to God. This is what Jesus had in mind when he told the impotent man who had been healed, "Behold, thou art made whole; sin no more, lest a worse thing come unto thee."[3] The faith to be committed forever to the work and purpose of God is infinitely more significant than the faith to be healed of physical infirmities.

THE MIND OF CHRIST

As we come to have real faith in God and in Christ Jesus, our Lord, we realize that we need to see life as Jesus sees it, but that it is not possible for us to do this all at once. Nor do we achieve the essentially Christian point of view by means of our own careful thinking. Indeed, cultivation of the mind of Christ is a lifelong and challenging task. It is won only in the refining experiences of true worship, when we bring the richest treasures and most persistent endeavors of heart and mind to the task of discovering God's will in his presence. We have yet to learn deeper meaning in the prayer of Jesus, "Father, if thou be willing, remove this cup from me; nevertheless, not my will, but thine be done."[4] Faith in God requires that the heart and mind be attuned to discover life's purpose through the act of worship, and nourishes the courage to translate that purpose in terms of the daily task.

Faith is inseparably connected with high morality. It demands complete moral devotion. Very often young people persuade their friends, and even themselves, that they cannot have full faith in Christianity because of their doubts regarding miracles or other aspects of the gospel. Often these young people, like the rich young ruler or the woman at the well, have run up against a moral snag — and the objection to which they point is rationalization — a kind of intellectual smoke screen designed to protect questionable moral practices and a consequent unwillingness to take up the cross. Such people lack faith, in the sense that they lack sufficient trust in God to adopt his standard for life in place of their own. They are in danger of the worst condemnation that can come to any man — which is, that in the presence of Christ he shall discover heights which he dare not climb.

The experience of ceasing to rebel against God — either deliberately or by indifference to his purpose in us — and of turning to him in faithful acceptance of his way of life is the foundation of forgiveness and reconciliation. Hitherto we have denied the purpose of God by our attitudes of rebellion or self-sufficiency; but now we seek to give him right-of-way in our lives. Hitherto, in spite of his great love for us, we were estranged from God. Hitherto we were held guilty of our sins, for we were continuing in sin; but now that we have come to hate sin, and are eager to put it away from us, we are "justified by faith."[5] We have exchanged the attitude of the Pharisee for that of the Publican.[6] "Being justified by faith, we have peace with God."[7] There is still much to do, but our relationship to God has changed with the change in our attitude. We are freed from guilt. This is not because we have earned our freedom, but because, once we take this attitude toward sin for our very own, God holds nothing against us.

Divine forgiveness is available to even the worst of us, and even the best of us need it. Christ readily forgave the promiscuous woman, the publican, the thief upon the cross, and many others. The particular form of their sinning was of secondary consequence; what was primary was that they were untrue to the purpose of God in their lives and so were traitors to their own well-being. In this sense we are all as needy as they were. But because of the love of God none of us need fear to seek the forgiveness which they sought and found. And none of us need forgiveness so much as one who thinks he has no need of it.

JUSTIFICATION BY GRACE

At the beginning of the Latter Day movement the church affirmed that "We know that justification through the grace of our Lord and Savior Jesus Christ, is just and true."[8] In this experience the church was in line with the great experiences of Paul and Luther and of many others.[9] But such "justification" (the acceptance and forgiveness of sinful men by God as if they were worthy of such love), and the remission of guilt and penalty because of a love-induced change of heart and mind, must not be separated from the experiences of repentance and baptism and the endowment of the Spirit.

There are other steps in the process of forgiveness in addition to justification, but the doctrine of justification emphasizes the first and most important of these: that as sinners we were at enmity against God, but that as soon as we truly accept him the enmity is done away. When the "middle wall

175

of partition"[10] has been broken down we are ready to move forward in the tasks of life with God. A truly great spiritual experience awaits us, if it is not already ours, when the Spirit of God burns into our hearts that which was in the heart of John as he wrote:

> As many as received him, to them gave he power to become the sons of God; only to them who believe on his name.[11]
> Whosoever drinketh of the water which I shall give him shall never thirst; but the water that I shall give him shall be in him a well of water springing up into everlasting life.[12]
> These [things] are written, that ye might believe that Jesus is the Christ, the son of God; and that believing ye might have life through his name.[13]
> Behold, I stand at the door, and knock; if any man hear my voice, and open the door, I will come in to him, and will sup with him, and he with me.[14]

From our side of the chasm created by sin, the first step toward reconciliation with God is to have faith in him: to trust him enough to follow him.

1. Ps. 146:3.
2. II Cor. 5:7; see also D. and C. 42:13.
3. John 5:14.
4. Luke 22:42.
5. Rom. 3:28.
6. Luke 18:10-14.
7. Rom. 5:1.
8. D. and C. 17:6 b.
9. Rom. 3:24-31; Gal. 2:16.
10. Eph. 2:14.
11. John 1:12.
12. John 4:16.
13. John 20:31.
14. Rev. 3:20.

22 | The Response of Repentance

FOR PURPOSES of discussion and emphasis we are analyzing the response of the individual to the love of God in terms of faith and repentance — in that order. Yet these overlap rather than follow each other in strict logical sequence. Indeed, they are so closely related that it is impossible to consider them fully in complete distinction from each other. They are both aspects of the same total experience, the emphasis in faith being on our attitude toward God and the emphasis in repentance being on our attitude toward sin.

So long as we remain in sin we are like pirate ships at war with the legitimate shipping on the high seas. When we are won by the overtures of divine love, we do not seek pardon because piracy does not pay, but because we have come to hate it. We enlist in the maritime service because we want to take our rightful place in the spiritual commerce of our times, and because we have complete confidence in the great Commander who directs the entire fleet. We are still the captains of our own souls, but we command our souls under orders from above. Far from resenting these orders, we seek them. They make it possible to coordinate our movements with those of other vessels, and from the basis of our own thought and action. Moreover, in following instructions from above we gradually learn the purpose of those instructions, enter into

177

the spirit of the entire action of life, share the mind of our Commander, and grow in spiritual stature and wisdom.

CHANGE OF PURPOSE

The change of heart from rebellion to obedience we have called "faith." It is essentially an act of confidence in the Commander. The change of life from piracy to service we have called "repentance."

In the Old Testament the word which has been translated "repent" means to turn or to return. In the New Testament the Greek words which are translated "repent" and "repentance" seem to place foremost the idea of a change of mind or a change of purpose. Jesus always related repentance to the love of God and the coming of his kingdom. We may therefore regard repentance as turning away from sin because of a new vision of the love of God and the glory of his kingdom. It is closely related to "conversion," which involves the idea of turning away or turning over or changing the form.

Noteworthy illustrations of true repentance are found in Job when out of the depths of humility he said, "I abhor myself, and repent in dust and ashes"[1]; or in David as he prayed to the Lord the great psalm of repentance, "Create in me a clean heart, O God; and renew a right spirit within me"[2]; or in the parable of the prodigal son where after the son "came unto himself" he said, "I will arise and go to my Father."[3] In each of these examples the repentant sinner turns away from his old self and his old sinfulness. While this will include turning from specific sins, it goes much further. It means the abandonment of a life of rebellion.

Whenever the repentant sinner discovers a place at which his life is out of harmony with the life and purpose of God, he is already committed to a change of life at that point. There is a parallel in our practice of scrutinizing communications presented to the church as revelations from God. We examine

178

these communications to see if they bear the evidences of Divinity. If they do, then as servants of God we are already committed to receiving them. In much the same way, the man who loves God examines his own life daily. If he finds that it is out of harmony with the divine will, he is already committed to its abandonment. When Job, David, and the prodigal son recognized that all sin is hateful, and registered their eternal enmity against it, they had obeyed one of the basic conditions of divine forgiveness.

Repentance necessarily involves pain. Because of this, people of smaller caliber who are unwilling to face the travail out of which a higher life is born hide themselves from the voice of God and never come to the humility and dignity of repentance. Lacking the courage and the incentive for even self-criticism, they become opinionated, dogmatic, intolerant, and more eager for good opinion than for facts.

Repentance is not merely admitting a few shortcomings or even expressing contrition for them. The confession, "I have sinned," was made by a heart-hardened Pharaoh,[4] a double-minded Balaam,[5] a remorseful Achan,[6] an insincere King Saul,[7] and a despairing Judas,[8] but in no one of these cases does there seem to have been true repentance. In true repentance we take God's part against ourselves, have sympathy with God, feel how unworthily the Ruler, Father, and Friend of men has been treated, and commit ourselves to his way. It does not ask, "What will my sin bring to me?" but "What does my sin mean to God?" It involves, in addition to mere recognition of sin, an emotional element, a change of feeling, sorrow for sins committed against goodness and justice and therefore hateful to God and hateful in itself.[9]

ACKNOWLEDGE SIN

For the sake of clearness let us consider some of the major aspects of genuine repentance, remembering that these overlap constantly and are just one experience viewed from several different angles.

179

The first requirement of effective repentance is that we shall recognize sin for what it is, and be genuinely sorry for it. We shall do this only as we have faith in God and sense something of the blackness of sin in contrast with the beauty of holiness. This is a soul-searching experience, especially for a person who has been proud of his moral standards. Our natural tendency is to avoid this experience as too painful, to gloss over the fact of sin, calling it by other names and excusing ourselves for our part in it. The man who is genuinely repentant does not do this. Nor does he condemn himself as utterly unworthy. But he does face the facts, and he faces them against the background of the love of God. He does his utmost to see sin as God sees it and to take toward it the attitude which God takes. There is no attempt to excuse or defend it. The repentant man sits in judgment on his own wrongdoings, judges fairly and impartially, and pronounces sentence on his sinning. There is only one sentence: by the grace of God our sin must be eradicated as soon as possible and as fully as possible.

This first step in repentance is made particularly difficult by the fact that both habit and conscience join the attempt to justify us in our sinning. We say, "I have always done it that way," or "Well, I was born that way." Conscience, which should accuse us, is frequently educated away from the truth, wasting its strength in reminding us of transgressions of social taboos while remaining silent when we transgress in the weightier matters of the law. If we need an example consider Jeremiah Mather, a prominent New England Christian whose wealth came from the slave traffic, but who was considered a model of piety and Christian devotion. He could not see beyond the conventional religion of his day.

While on first thought repentance may seem to be easy, in actual fact it is only possible as God shall go with us every step of the way, opening our eyes to clear vision and steeling our souls to honor and courage. The big problem is not to deal with our penitence, but to deal with that impenitence which masquerades in the garb of righteousness. For practically all of us, our besetting sins are walled around by custom and consent. We have become so habituated to overlooking these sins that we do not recognize their true nature, until the grace of God, with our consent, forces us to face the fact of our own wrongdoings.

It has been said of man: "As he thinketh in his heart, so is he."[10] The heart is an unusual place to do one's thinking. The counsel is phrased in this way because we need to recognize the tremendous influence of our interests on our thinking. This counsel should be considered with a statement of the Master, "Where your treasure is, there will your heart be also."[11] The big businessman, passionately eager for business success, will be influenced in his thinking by that passion, and will justify himself in actions which an onlooker will regard as entirely unjustifiable. A statesman like Bismarck will confess, "We do things in the service of His Majesty which we would not think of doing as private citizens." His interest has warped his moral perceptions. There are countless illustrations of the same tendency in our own daily life. Our investments control our attitudes unless we are wide awake to the danger of self-delusion and have the courage to face it. In many situations unequivocal facing of our own bias is essential to straight thinking. And quite frequently this straight thinking cannot proceed until we admit clearly and flatly that we have been wrong, and that nothing can justify what we have done.

The way of righteousness is the way of truth — truth about God and truth about ourselves. We can never be at one with God until we realize this and act upon it. It will not do to hide our heads in the sand, for our sins cannot be escaped that way. In spite of the pain of it, we must face the fact of our sinfulness just as an intelligent man faces the truth

181

about the cancer which threatens to kill him. In the other way there is no hope, but in this way there is hope.

The truth I am seeking to convey is especially important to intelligent and cultured people. Such people find it very difficult to think of themselves as sinners. Indeed, one of their major characteristics is their spiritual complacency. When we mention sin they retreat behind the walls of their conscious respectability as a medieval knight retreated behind the walls of his castle. They do not know the meaning of repentance because they are so proud of what they have in their heads that they will not, or cannot, look honestly at what is in their hearts.

ACCEPT RESPONSIBILITY

A further requirement which is laid on us by our very natures and by that of God is that, having faced our sin squarely and recognized it for what it is, we shall accept responsibility for it. This is difficult, for we live in an age of alibis in which the manufacture of excuses has been elevated to a high art. We are more adept than any prior generation at dodging responsibility. We blame our heredity, our environment, our subconscious life, the pressure of the economic order, our neighbors, or — if we must get back to Adam — our wives; anything and anyone so long as we ourselves are not caught.

Psychiatrists tell us that thousands of people seek refuge from the realities of daily living in daydreams. When life becomes too arduous some dwell in their daydreams so completely that they believe their dreams rather than reality. James Thurber wrote a classic short story about Walter Mitty, a man who found refuge from an unsatisfactory reality by escaping to a glorious world of fantasy and imagination. When in real life a man gets to this point, and thinks that he is Napoleon or Rockefeller or the king of the cannibal islands, we send him up to an institution and say that he is insane; but all of us do it to a greater or lesser degree despite

182

the fact that nothing can change our basic responsibility for our action.

No man can take the first step toward repentance who is continually on the defensive against God. That is even more foolish than being on the defensive against one's doctor. Our Father does not seek to convict us of sin so as to condemn us, but to save us; and there is no salvation which will endure except a salvation based on the truth.

Genuine repentance is a sane and healthy necessity for the average man: a square facing of facts, without alibiing and without attempting to avoid responsibility. It is not just that we have "made a few mistakes" or that we "did our best but that wasn't good enough," or that we did what "anyone else would have done." We must face the fact of our willful wrongdoing — our sin — and accept responsibility for doing rightly. In this way lies strength and power; for the vigor which was previously given to avoiding facts now goes to changing them, and the friendships which were once destroyed by resentment are now won by honesty. The man who accepts the responsibility for his sins differs from the man who seeks forgiveness so that he can forget his sins as much as chalk differs from cheese.

EAGER TO MAKE REPARATION

Beyond all question true repentance includes eagerness to make reparation. Jesus has taught us to see sin in its social consequences. We cannot journey far with him until we recognize that every act of ours, whether it be good or ill, involves our heavenly Father, our neighbors, and ourselves. There can therefore be no true repentance which seeks to right the relationship between us and God but leaves our neighbors out of the picture. For a man to seek forgiveness and yet be content to leave others to suffer the consequences of his ill-doing is to perpetuate the same selfish indifference to others which is at the very heart of the sin which he is supposed to be

183

forsaking. To do this is to repent of a specific act, but to continue the ungodly habit of indifference toward his brother's good. This is not true repentance, but spiritual blindness. God can have no interest in such an attitude. Whenever he leads a man toward genuine repentance, part of that experience is eagerness to make reparation for the mischief which has been wrought.

When sin has been committed on the purely material plane reparation is generally easy. Yet even here a certain lavish generosity is required in estimating the consequences of dishonesty and oppression. The money which was stolen or the oppression which was practiced, may have led to far-reaching results such as cannot now be measured in material terms. Zaccheus attempted to practice such generosity when he offered to refund fourfold that which he had taken by fraud.[12] But if reparation on this plane is difficult, reparation on a higher plane may be impossible without divine aid.

This is illustrated forcefully in George Eliot's story, *Adam Bede*. In this story we meet Donnithorne — careless, impulsive, well-meaning, rich — who had taken advantage of the girl Adam Bede loved. After the shame of bearing Donnithorne's child, the girl lost her mind. Brought to himself, the young man tried desperately to make amends. He finally faced Adam, who forgave him. But Adam reminded Donnithorne that even when all is forgiven, "There's a sort o' damage, sir, that can't be made up for." No reparations which Donnithorne might offer could undo what he had done. Indeed since only God could know what might have been, only God could counteract the far-ranging consequences of sin.

Here, again, we are brought back to the point at which we constantly find ourselves. Any meaningful approach to God is a response to his search for us. Any effective repentance must be made under his guidance. Beyond this, it is the faith and testimony of the church that through the grace of the Lord Jesus Christ sinners can be won to faith and

184

repentance, and to restitution and rebuilding, out of which shall come, in time, the fulfillment of the divine purpose in us.

---

1. Job 42:6.
2. Ps. 51:10.
3. Luke 15:18.
4. Ex. 9:27.
5. Num. 22:34.
6. Josh. 7:20.
7. I Sam. 15:24.
8. Matt. 27:4.
9. A. H. Strong, *Systematic Theology* (Westwood, New Jersey: Fleming H. Revell Company, 1954), p. 832.
10. Prov. 23:7.
11. Matt. 6:21.
12. Luke 19:8.

23 | Conversion and the New Birth

WE MUST NOW INQUIRE concerning the manner in which one becomes a disciple of the Lord Jesus Christ. Rarely, if ever, is this an instantaneous experience. Nevertheless, there has to be a time of decision and commitment. For many Christian people this decision is *conversion*. Conversion has been described as

> the reorientation of the soul of an individual, the deliberate turning from indifference or from an earlier form of piety to another, a turning which implies a consciousness that a great change is involved, that the old was wrong and the new is right.[1]

The features of such conversion have been classified by William James as

> a passion of willingness and acquiescence, which removes the feeling of anxiety, a sense of perceiving truths not known before, a sense of clean and beautiful newness within and without and an ecstasy of happiness.[2]

CONVERSION AND INTEGRATION

A high percentage of conversions takes place in adolescence. This is not difficult to understand. The physical birth is not a moral birth. As modern revelation indicates, a child is not fully "accountable." He comes into the world a little

186

animal, his impelling motives being his as yet unmodified and uncontrolled instincts which play upon him and dominate his life. The great task of his early life is the formation of a true self, who shall be the master and not the tool of his instincts and impulses. He must learn to be self-guided in the sense that his activity is determined, as fully as may be, by purposes and ideals. During this period he is not yet truly a person, but a complex of competing characteristics. He cannot become a man until one group of harmonious purposes become dominant in his life. Without such pervasive purpose, such reason for existence, he is not a man but a walking civil war. He cannot be his own man, or anyone else's man in any final sense, until he finds integrity through devotion to a person or a cause.[3]

I have said that most conversions take place in adolescence. This is because adolescence is the natural period of evaluation and commitment. From the moral point of view, all that has taken place hitherto is preparation for entrance into adulthood with its responsibilities and commitments. But there are many conversions later in life. This is particularly true when the earlier orientation of the personality was around an inadequate purpose for which a new center of personality is now substituted. The significant fact is that at the time or in the process of conversion the life which was divided and frustrated becomes united and purposeful.

It is of the nature of conversion that it involves the whole man. This is indicated, so far as the Christian is concerned, by the first and greatest commandment: "Thou shalt love the Lord thy God with all they heart and with all thy soul, and with all thy mind, and with all thy strength."[4] If anyone worships a false god, he needs to be converted (turned around) to the worship of the true God. Less evident, but equally true, is the fact that if anyone worships with less than his whole heart, might, mind, and strength, then he, too, needs conversion. His life is misdirected because of his

187

divided loyalties, and can be set in the right direction only by the integration of his loyalties.

This integration of the entire personality is a deeply emotional experience. William James has likened it to falling in love with Jesus.[5] But it is insecure if it is merely an emotional experience. As the Master indicated, the mind and the will must be equally involved with the heart. The importance of this full involvement becomes evident when we consider the high percentage of backslidings among those who were "converted" under strong emotional pressures. Despite this caution it is important to remember that there are many, many amazing life changes which can only be explained as the expression of a new love. The onetime outcast has fallen in love with Jesus, and so has fallen out of love with his past way of life. Without love there is no conversion.

While the conversion experience has both affirmative and negative aspects, it is essentially affirmative. The convert who is deeply disturbed by his sin and guilt is so disturbed because he has heard the voice of Jesus and has come to believe that the Lord Jesus is calling him to begin a new life and will stand by him as he takes up this new life. There are many accounts of conversion in the scriptures, but in all of them the affirmative aspect is preeminent. It is not sin and misery which occupy the center of the stage but the winning Person of Jesus Christ.

TYPES OF CONVERSIONS

The book of Acts is a book of confrontations and beginnings. It would not be sound to presume that none of the men and women we meet here had heard of Jesus before they appear in Luke's story, but they had never before met Jesus in the full splendor of his resurrection, wherein he had been declared in no unmistakable terms to be the Son of God.[6] Accordingly, we may expect to find in Acts many stories of what happened as a result of a new and startlingly impressive awareness of Jesus, and we do.

The second chapter of Acts tells of the Day of Pentecost, and of the change of heart which came to those who heard Peter's presentation of the claims of the Lord Jesus, and who felt the spirit of the One whom Peter proclaimed. Later it tells of the conversion of the Negro eunuch, after his eyes had been opened under the ministry of Philip; of Cornelius the centurion, whose conversion was made possible after both he and Peter had been specially prepared from heaven; of Saul of Tarsus, whose life was completely redirected after his vision of the risen Christ on the way to Damascus; of Sergius Paulus, and of the jailer at Thessalonica; of "certain disciples" from Ephesus; and of many Jews and proselytes who are not mentioned by name. In all of these cases where any details are given we get an impression of conversion as a sharp and dramatic thing.

In the Gospels we meet such early saints as Levi, the publican,[7] and Mary Magdalene, who seem to have been converted in movingly dramatic fashion. But we also meet Andrew, Peter, Thomas, John, Nathaniel, and others, whose coming-into-awareness was a much more gradual thing. They had their times of decision, but we can see many of them proceeding from understanding to understanding, so that even before the resurrection threw its flood of light into their hearts and minds they had begun to be new men through Christ. Later we meet Timothy, Paul's "son in the gospel," and are specifically told that the unfeigned faith that was in him had dwelt first in his grandmother, Lois, and in his mother, Eunice.[8]

There is no significant difference between these two types of converts — those who came to their experience of discipleship with surprising suddenness, and those who came to the same experience after a more gradual approach to the point of climax. Careful examination of the evidence in these cases seems to show that even such dramatic conversions as that of Paul himself were preceded by extended periods of preparation. The only suddenness about these experiences was the collapse of opposition to the divine entreaty. How powerfully Paul must have been influenced by the lives of the good men whom he persecuted and, more particularly, by the courageous death of Stephen!

In view of the evidence of the scriptures and of our own experience it is unfortunate that there has been a tendency at times to regard the dramatic experience as the only true type of conversion. It is certainly a valid type, and it is marvelous in our eyes. But it is not the only type, nor is that conversion which takes place gradually and in the course of the unfolding of life any less sure or any less divinely motivated than the more colorful experience.

It is quite likely that in the early years of the Christian dispensation a definite experience of conversion was presumed of candidates for baptism. This was to be expected, since the price of discipleship was so high in terms of readjustment and social ostracism. Yet the many references to the principle of calling and conversion which we find in the Book of Mormon and in modern revelation indicate that while circumstances may make conversion more apparent against some backgrounds than against others, the fact of conversion — of deliberately choosing for God, and committing one's life to him — is fundamental to the Christian way of life.

THE NEW BIRTH

Another term used to denote the beginnings of the Christian way of life and almost synonymous with conversion is "new birth." Whereas conversion emphasizes the new direction of the life of a believer, new birth stresses the new inspiration and power and quality of this life. New birth recognizes that if men such as we are to overcome sin we must become men after a new order. As Jesus himself said, we must be "born again."[9] And, as the apostle Paul said later, nothing else matters but that the man in Christ shall be in fact a "new creature."[10] In the whole history of ethical discussion there

190

is no saying more full of insight into the nature of the moral life than the words of Jesus, "Ye must be born again."[11]

Like conversion, the new birth stands in sharp contrast with any scheme of culture or of moral reform. It means that for the newborn, sin is henceforth branded with its true name and is regarded as an enemy. Neither education nor reform will do away with it. Sin cannot be improved, for the difficulty is with its very nature; it can only be abandoned. While education can do wonders for a man whose heart is right with God, it is completely beside the point, so far as God is concerned, unless and until this change of heart actually takes place.

Birth according to the flesh is ordinary human birth. It is the beginning of the human life which all of us know, under the conditions of sin which we have examined earlier in our studies. In parallel fashion, the new birth is the beginning of life in the family of God. Thus Peter speaks of the saints as having been "born again, not of corruptible seed, but of incorruptible, by the word of God."[12] John says that "to all who received him, who believed in his name, he gave power to become children of God; who were born, not of blood nor of the will of the flesh nor of the will of man, but of God."[13] And the apostle Paul, speaking from the Christian side of his conversion experience, wrote, "I am crucified with Christ; nevertheless I live; yet not I, but Christ liveth in me."[14]

The new birth, like conversion, is the work of God. It cannot be commanded; it can only be accepted. It is not the fruit of our insight, but of the operation of the love of God. It is not won by painful effort on our part, except as this is necessary to the abandonment of our willfulness and our rebellion. It is the gift of God, wrought by the power of God. We cannot be such persons as God leads us to see we ought to be except as we are born again from above.

In the new birth the distinctive emphasis is entirely forward looking. In a sermon whose fame has lasted more than a hundred years, Dr. Thomas Chalmers said:

191

There are two ways in which a practical moralist may attempt to displace from the human heart its love of the world—either by a demonstration of the world's vanity, so that the heart shall be prevailed upon simply to withdraw its regards from an object that is not worthy of it; or by setting forth another object, even God, as more worthy of its attachment, so that the heart shall be prevailed upon, not to resign an old affection which shall have nothing to succeed it, but to exchange an old affection for a new one. . . . From the constitution of our nature, the former method is altogether incompetent and ineffectual. . . . The latter method will alone suffice for the rescue and recovery of the heart from the wrong affection that domineers over it.[15]

This new birth, born of love, is the work of the Holy Spirit and is a prelude to a new way of life which is also guided by the Holy Spirit. Only in this new life, centering in the love of God, can we bring forth the works of righteousness which are accepted of God — the love offerings of our grateful hearts. As Jesus himself said: "A good tree cannot bring forth evil fruit; neither can a corrupt tree bring forth good fruit."[16] But a life lived toward God and by the power of God is secure in all its deeper values.

1. A. D. Nock, *Conversion*, p. 7, Oxford University Press.
2. *Ibid*, pp. 7, 8.
3. See James B. Pratt, *The Religious Consciousness*, Macmillan, pp. 122, 123.
4. Mark 12:35.
5. *Varieties of Religious Experience*, pp. 174, 175.
6. Rom. 1:4.
7. Luke 5:27.
8. II Tim. 1:5.
9. John 3:3.
10. Gal. 6:15.
11. James B. Pratt, *The Religious Consciousness*.
12. I Pet. 1:23.
13. John 1:12, 13, R.S.V.
14. Gal. 2:20.
15. "The Expulsive Power of a New Affection," quoted in *Master Sermons of the Nineteenth Century*, Gaius Glenn Atkins, p. 4.
16. Matt. 7:27.

24 Baptism and the Divine Purpose

THE DIVINE PURPOSE for men includes all mankind. It is for "every nation, and kindred, and tongue, and people."[1] It cannot be achieved until those who "in times past were not a people" become "the people of God."[2] And "a people" is more than an association of individuals. A people have common interests and goals and spirit and character. They belong together and can be distinguished from other peoples who have different interests and goals and spirit and character.

The divine purpose in man can only be fulfilled in and through twice-born men who together belong to the people who constitute the family of God. When a man is born again he is born into this family. His repentance from his onetime self-centeredness is not complete until he has abandoned his isolation and entered into the life of the family of God.

There are many reasons for this. Every man needs the affectionate support of his fellows, and every man also needs a family group who depend on him. This uncalculated alternation of dependence and ministry in the family makes a family one of the most potent character-shaping agencies that there is, and is ordained of God. The new birth is therefore more than an individual experience. It is a great event in the life of the family of God. It adds new strength and broadens the area of affectionate concern and cooperation. What the individual members of the family might have lacked in courage

193

and spirit and the enduring will to do, they can now do in concert with their brethren, each supplying something unique, and everyone being loved first as a brother and only secondarily as a contributor. The gifts which he brings to the life of the family are accepted with gratitude as being determined by the character and wisdom of the Father, even "those members of the body, which seem to be more feeble" being important parts of the family life.[3]

PENTECOST

The necessary union of men of faith was illustrated on the day of Pentecost. On that occasion there was a great gathering of Jews who had consented to the crucifixion of the Lord Jesus Christ. They came together as scoffers, but under the guidance of the Holy Spirit Peter helped them to see truly what had happened at Calvary, and the love of God which had prompted the sacrifice of his Son on that lonely hill. Forgetful of the fears which had at one time restrained him, Peter said boldly: "Let all the house of Israel know assuredly, that God hath made that same Jesus whom ye have crucified, both Lord and Christ,"[4] and, wonder of wonders, they believed him. Being "pricked in their hearts" they cried out, "Men and brethren, what shall we do?"[5]

Peter answered, as might be expected, that those who now saw what God had done for them, and what they had done to the Son of God, should repent. This was reasonable and obvious. But Peter followed this admonition with a command that those who were repentant should now be baptized. And for fear anyone should imagine himself to be exempt from this requirement, the apostle said,

> Repent, and be baptized *every one of you* in the name of Jesus Christ, for the remission of sins, and ye shall receive the gift of the Holy Ghost. For the promise is unto *you, and to your children,* and to *all that are afar off, even as many as the Lord our God shall call.*[6]

194

The men who listened to Peter and his fellow apostles were in deadly earnest. They now knew themselves to be murderers of the worst kind, for they had sinned against both light and love. Nothing could now undo what they had done, and yet they could never rest so long as their guilty knowledge lay heavy on their consciences. Peter understood this, for he himself had known a time when it seemed he could not live with the memory of his cowardly denial in Gethsemane and the Judgment Hall. Out of his own experience he did not offer to leave men some chance to work out their debt. He knew that there was no way in which this could possibly be done. But he did invite them to accept the divine mercy, and from hearts filled with the wonder of the forgiveness offered to them so freely, to enlist in the cause of Christ, under the banner of Christ, and in fraternal alliance with the disciples of Christ.

The heart of the Christian message is that "where sin abounded, grace did much more abound."[7] This is what filled the heart of Peter and was the core of his message. He was talking to Jews who had considered themselves as the chosen people, but who now knew that they had been untrue to their heritage. That the people chosen to prepare the way of the Lord should kill the looked-for Messiah without cause was the worst sin conceivable. But Peter announced that even this condemnation could not stand before the onslaughts of the grace of God. The Father had provided the Sacrifice by whose life and death, and in whose Spirit, they were now awakened to their condition and their need and their responsibility. They must repent, and they must join the fellowship of the repentant; and when they did this with full purpose of heart the Spirit which they had seen manifest in the life of Jesus, and which they now felt in their hearts, would bear constant witness of the love and mercy of God and would remain with them as their guide and inspiration in the new life to which they were now called together.

195

The repentance to which Peter called the Jews was not merely godly sorrow. Indeed, it did not center in the responsibility which they carried because they had consented to the murder of the Lord Jesus. It required an awareness of their situation — that they should see the life that they had lived in its true dimensions and consequences; but their eyes had been opened by Calvary's revelation of the love of God in Christ, and Peter's primary concern was with their response to this love. He was thinking of their tomorrows, not of their yesterdays. He was proclaiming "repentance unto life."[8]

It was as though Peter had said, "Now that your eyes are opened, and your hearts are warmed, turn your backs on the sin which crucifies the Lord of Glory and give him the love of your hearts and the service of your hands. Change from the service of the lesser gods and devote your allegiance to Almighty God. When you do this you will find that the Lord Jesus will accept you and will cleanse you and will commission you. When you find yourselves entrusted with your share of the task for which Christ died and in which his disciples are now being enlisted, then, and only then, will you know that you have been truly forgiven."

The words of the apostle Peter at Pentecost were in full harmony with the demands of the situation and with the commission which all the apostles had received from the Master: "Go ye into all the world, and preach the gospel to every creature. He that believeth and is baptized, shall be saved; but he that believeth not, shall be damned."[9] It was true then, and it is true today, that he who accepts at face value the divine offer of forgiveness and enlists in the cause which he once opposed by his actions or by his indifference finds in this enlistment the fulfillment of the divine purpose in him and the joy which comes with this sense of fulfillment. But, on the other hand, he who will not accept a junior partnership in the work of God is damned. That is what damnation

196

is. It is choosing to remain in darkness when one might have lived in the light.

THE NECESSITY FOR BAPTISM

Although the experience of Pentecost was an outstanding one, this was not the only occasion when repentance, the remission of sins, and rebirth were directly associated with baptism in the apostolic church. There were many such occasions, one of them occurring when the gospel was first taken to the Gentiles.

It was hard for the Jews of the apostolic age to realize that the gospel is intended for men of every nation, for they had been taught to believe that salvation is essentially for the Jews. Even Peter had to have special preparation before he realized that his acceptance with God depended on his willingness to accept as partners in the work of God all those whom God should choose. This special preparation came to Peter when he was at prayer in the house of Simon, a tanner who lived at Joppa. During this worship Peter was caused to know that he should not despise any whom God should choose. In this way he was prepared to minister to Cornelius, a devout man who feared God and gave alms to the poor, whose messengers sought out Peter even while the apostle was at prayer. Three days later Peter stood with his companions in the home of Cornelius and told the Gentiles of the good news of the gospel. As he preached, the testimony of the Spirit accompanied his words. The gifts of the Holy Ghost were poured out on those present and they spoke with tongues and magnified God; and Peter, his eyes opened wide for the first time, commanded these Gentiles to be baptized in the name of the Lord.[10]

By ordinary standards Cornelius was already a man of God. Although he was a Roman of high authority, he was both devout and generous. But the messenger sent to him

197

from God was quite evidently aware that Cornelius needed to go further. He needed to be included in the company of the saints, and that which included him was the rite of baptism. As truly as faith affects something, and repentance affects something, so also baptism affects something: it is a positive ethical factor in salvation; it has moral power and significance; it belongs to the conversion experience. It is a prerequisite of the kind of salvation that Christianity seeks to give. It gives body and substance and outreach to that which would otherwise be shadowy and anemic and circumscribed.

In the New Testament the new birth is constantly associated with baptism. Nowadays there is a tendency to disparage this and similar ordinances and to say that at best they are permissive, and never obligatory. But this is not true to the facts. Before conversion, sin has taken a very strong hold on us. It is not only an attitude of mind; it is a physical appetite. It is altogether fitting, therefore, that the conditions which we must obey in order that the life of God may flow into our lives shall include some such physical act as baptism. Baptism by immersion is not merely an outward sign of an inward grace, but it is part of the total experience of adjusting heart and mind and body to the authority of God so that his life can flow without impediment into every part of our lives.

People beyond number have permitted their Christianity to be shipwrecked simply because they are not vitally attached to the organic life of the people of God. One of the most insidious temptations of the devil is the temptation to continue in isolation, imagining that a personal relationship with God is possible without a resultant relationship with his people. To yield to this temptation is itself a sin. The essence of this thought is admirably expressed by Dr. Charles Clayton Morrison, who says:

> The typical evangelism which obtains in our day is censorable for its lack of the baptismal note. Our evangelism

preaches faith and repentance but is afraid of baptism. It awakens religious aspirations but fails to carry these impulses into social objectivity. The implications of its gospel are that confession is an experience between the soul and God, and as a result many a soul imagines it is converted and saved when it has simply experienced a shower bath of its own emotions . . . there is need—profound and crying need—of that evangelism which, when men cry out to know what to do, is not afraid to proclaim Peter's pentecostal word: "Repent and be baptized . . . for the remission of your sins." For men are saved by baptism as truly as by faith and repentance.[11]

The demand of our day is for some definite assurance of salvation which is more than a mere emotional experience. Nowadays, as in apostolic times, people are asking, "What shall we *do?*" Pentecost offers the answer today, just as it did twenty centuries ago, because the basic need of men and women is unchanged. When sinners are convinced that the Jesus whom they have each crucified is indeed the Son of God, when they realize that their lesser sins all grow out of the parent sin of rebellion against God, and when they want some definite assurance that these things shall not be held against them — then we must give them some answer which calls for definite and specific action, just as Peter offered repentance and baptism to the men of his time. It may be that we shall never be able to explain all that is involved in repentance, in baptism for the remission of sins, and in the gift of the Holy Ghost, but we can follow the way pointed out, giving our intelligent and whole-souled surrender at each step of the way. In doing this we will experience that which transformed the lives of the early disciples and changed the course of history. The definite act of baptism, according to Peter, was to give assurance to the sinner that his past transgressions were wiped out, and that he was now trusted with the life and the secrets of the Christian community. No real or fancied growth during the intervening centuries has done away with the need for just such an act, and for just such a purpose.

The symbolism of baptism by immersion in water is clear and comprehensive. Perhaps the most obvious symbol is that of cleansing. Sin is unclean and impure. Its stain is no imaginary thing, but is a dark blot which brands and disfigures. Lady Macbeth, wandering through the corridors of the castle night after night washing, washing, washing the hand stained with murder, is a picture of guilt which cannot be denied. For those who sense their guilt, there are only two possible solutions: bitter and hopeless despair, or some evidence of divine cleansing. No one can wash himself clean of responsibility for sin by any act of public disclaimer, but the sinner can be washed clean by the free and gracious action of a loving Father.

The drama of cleansing at the hands of God, however, does not exhaust the symbolic significance of the baptismal rite. The apostle Paul, who had himself been baptized in fulfillment of a divine command,[12] was quick to see an even richer symbolism than the one baptizing him had perceived. Out of this richer understanding he wrote to the saints in Rome:

> Know ye not, that so many of us as were baptized into Jesus Christ were baptized into his death? Therefore we are buried with him by baptism into death; that like as Christ was raised up from the dead by the glory of the Father, even so we also should walk in newness of life. For if we have been planted together in the likeness of his death, we shall be also in the likeness of his resurrection; knowing this, that our old man is crucified with him, that the body of sin might be destroyed, that henceforth we should not serve sin. For he that is dead to sin is freed from sin. Now if we be dead with Christ, we believe that we shall also live with him; knowing that Christ being raised from the dead dieth no more; death hath no more dominion over him. For in that he died, he died unto sin once; but in that he liveth, he liveth unto God. Likewise reckon ye also yourselves to be dead indeed unto sin, but alive unto God through Jesus Christ our Lord.[18]

It is no accident that this symbolism is so complete. There is no better means than baptism in water for impressing the significant facts of the total baptismal experience: death to sin, resurrection to righteousness, and new life, all of which are the gifts of God.

1. Rev. 14:6.
2. I Pet. 2:10.
3. I Cor. 12:22, Eph. 4.
4. Acts 2:36.
5. Acts 2:37.
6. Acts 2:38, 39.
7. Rom. 5:20.
8. Acts 11:18.
9. Mark 16:14, 15.
10. Acts 10:48.
11. *The Meaning of Baptism,* The Disciples' Publication Society (Chicago), p. 162.
12. Acts 22:16.
13. Rom. 6:3-11.

25 | The Spirit of Life

W E ARE CREATED by our heavenly Father and endowed with many gifts in order that we might use these for the achievement of his purposes in our creation; but instead we have used these gifts as though they were of our own devising and as though we have no responsibility beyond ourselves for the ends to which we employ them. Or, perhaps, we have acknowledged God after our fashion, but have given him no final authority in our lives, regarding him as a sort of absentee landlord who lurks as a dim figure in the background, but who does not have to be seriously considered in the affairs of our daily lives.

Whether we have lived in defiant rebellion against God, or merely in unresponsive ignorance of his loving purpose in us, or even in half-hearted acknowledgment and service, he has always loved us; and he still loves us and seeks our full and loving involvement in his way of life for our sakes. To this end he invites us to look honestly and steadily at what he has done for us; when we do this truly he knows that we shall be won by his love and shall come to love and trust him in return. He can then treat us on the basis of this love, remembering our transgressions against us no more,[1] and will share with us the joy and the labor which go with the salvation of his other children and which become the means to our own further salvation.[2]

As we have seen, it is just and proper that those who accept the Lord's offer of forgiveness and acceptance shall register their new allegiance in such a rite as baptism. By this sacred ordinance past sins are remitted because they are acknowledged and repudiated. The meaning and burden of them is changed because the onetime sinner is changed by the power of God.[3] A new relationship is set up in which our heavenly Father does not love us any more than he did previously, but in which his love becomes more effective because we are more responsive. This new relationship is not something to be achieved and then forgotten. It is infinitely intimate and precious, and should become more and more so from day to day. This is only possible as the Spirit of the Lord Jesus, which is the Spirit of God, is our constant guide and companion.

ENDOWMENT

When Jesus was about to leave his disciples, he told them that his Spirit would come to them as their Guide and Comforter.[4] His own character was to be theirs, as well as his method and way of life. Such was the impress of his personality on these faithful men that this actually took place. The early church became the church of an inspired people who were empowered by the Spirit of Christ both to know and to do his will. Dull as many of them had been, and hard of heart, they were transformed into new men who turned the world upside down with no weapon but love and trust.[5] As one of them put it, "The weapons of our warfare are not carnal, but mighty through God to the pulling down of strongholds."[6] And the chief of these weapons was the proclamation of the love of God which grants forgiveness to repentant sinners and calls them to share his own life. This is still the chief weapon in the armory of the Saints.

While the physical act of baptism is necessary as the means and symbol of entrance into life in the body of Christ, actual life in the body depends on the spirit of the members.

In a very real sense full membership in the body is not achieved until those who have made covenant with Christ in the waters of baptism have been so endowed with his Spirit that they are enabled to do his work in his way.[7] The beginning of the Christian church in Samaria, for example, emphasizes this close relation between baptism and the bestowal of the Holy Spirit. Philip had preached Christ in Samaria and had baptized a number of men and women. When Philip reported his success to the apostles in Jerusalem, the apostles sent Peter and John,

> who, when they were come down, prayed for them, that they might receive the Holy Ghost. (For as yet he was fallen upon none of them; only they were baptized in the name of the Lord Jesus.) Then laid they their hands on them, and they received the Holy Ghost.[8]

On the Maine coast a boy once asked an old sailor as he sat mending a sail, "What is the wind?" After thinking a little the old man answered, "I do not really know what the wind is, but I do know how to hoist a sail." In the same way it was not easy for the early church to explain the Holy Spirit; but they did learn how to put themselves in the way of endowment by the Spirit, and an unfailing mark of its coming was the receipt of power both to see and to do the will of God. The record of many marvelous things done under this Spirit and Power has been preserved to us, and it is altogether likely that many, many more went unrecorded. But the real significance of action under the Spirit did not lie in the doing of miracles. It lay, rather, in the sharing of light and power for life with God. The Holy Spirit taught and helped the disciples to live as Jesus lived. They were enabled to see in expanding proportion the true meaning of discipleship, to enter more and more fully into the purpose of God and to declare in convincing fashion the source of the power which they enjoyed.

The endowment of the Holy Spirit is available in the

fellowship of the Saints in this present age, even as it was in the apostolic age. It is this Spirit which makes the church the primary means in the hands of God for the achievement of his purpose, by the constant prophetic reinterpretation of this purpose in terms of the changing world scene, and by the quickening of the heart and mind and conscience of the Saints in that free obedience which is their life.

Despite the renunciation of the self-centered ways of life which the Spirit enjoins, life in the Spirit is a gladsome experience. Luke tells us that the early disciples were "filled with joy, and with the Holy Ghost."[9] Out of a Spirit-prompted desire to share his own happiness Paul prayed for the saints in Rome: "Now the God of hope fill you with all joy and peace in believing, that ye may abound in hope, through the power of the Holy Ghost."[10] This "joy unspeakable and full of glory,"[11] and its availability even in the midst of tribulations,[12] was a constant witness to the soundness of the Christian way, as it has been in every succeeding age.

COMMUNION

Although the change which is wrought in conversion, and which is registered in baptism, is a very real one, we do not thereby become perfect in a moment. We now fight against evil within and around us, and we fight with full assurance of victory, but the victory has not yet been won. We need to be reminded again and again of our heavenly Father's sacrifice of love in the person of his Son, and so to be persuaded again and again to do our utmost to live his life in the power of his Spirit.

Before his crucifixion, during their last meal together, the Lord Jesus provided the means by which men might be thus reminded:

> As they were eating, Jesus took bread and brake it, and blessed it, and gave to his disciples, and said, Take, eat; this

205

is in remembrance of my body, which I give a ransom for you. And he took the cup, and gave thanks, and gave it to them, saying, Drink ye all of it. For this is in remembrance of my blood of the new testament, which is shed for as many as shall believe on my name, for the remission of their sins.[13]

This rite of remembrance and renewal was from the first a family meal. The disciples ate the bread and drank the wine together and with their Lord in a solemn mutual covenant. After the resurrection, whenever the disciples met to partake of this covenant meal, it was still a family experience, and their leaders took special pains to see that the worshipers participated in the family spirit. With this in mind the apostle Paul told the saints in Corinth:

Whosoever shall eat this bread, and drink this cup of the Lord, unworthily, shall be guilty of the body and blood of the Lord. But let a man examine himself, and so let him eat of that bread, and drink of that cup. For he that eateth and drinketh unworthily, eateth and drinketh condemnation to himself, not discerning the Lord's body.[14]

Paul has expressed the spirit of the entire Christian enterprise in these sentences. The body of the Lord Jesus was in a unique sense one body, all its parts being "fitly joined together and compacted" by that which every part supplied.[15] That body was broken, and its life was spilled forth in loving sacrifice for the redemption of mankind. We must come back again and again to remember this redeeming truth, says Paul, and because of this remembrance the whole body of us — the body of Christ — must be united as his body, and broken and spilled forth in sacrificial service, even as his body was broken and spilled forth.

Paul was instructed in these things by the Lord himself,[16] who had taught the Jews in the synagogue at Capernaum,

Except ye eat the flesh of the Son of Man, and drink his

blood, ye have no life in you. Whoso eateth my flesh, and drinketh my blood, hath eternal life; and I will raise him up in the resurrection of the just at the last day. For my flesh is meat indeed, and my blood is drink indeed. He that eateth my flesh, and drinketh my blood, dwelleth in me, and I in him. As the living Father hath sent me, and I lived by the Father; so he that eateth me, even he shall live by me. This is that bread which came down from heaven; not as your fathers did eat manna, and are dead; he that eateth of this bread shall live for ever.[17]

It is probable that among Latter Day Saints the greatest single witness to the central importance of unity and forgiveness and dedication is the communion of the Lord's Supper. Our serious regard for this ordinance has been one of the most creative spiritual forces in our church life. This is probably because we have been led by the Spirit to take at face value such instructions as this:

If thou bring thy gift to the altar, and there rememberest that thy brother hath aught against thee, leave thou thy gifts before the altar, and go thy way unto thy brother, and first be reconciled to thy brother, and then come and offer thy gift.[18]

And, more recently, "If any have trespassed, let him not partake until he makes reconciliation."[19]

Broken bread and outpoured wine are quite simple things. Among worldly men they might easily be regarded as symbols of the basic disunity of mankind, for the chief cause of war down the generations has been greed for access to the basic materials of life.[20] But in the experience of the Saints bread and wine have taken on a very sacred meaning and are a constant reminder of the fashion in which God makes of things which have divided the means to unity. In this present day our joy in this meal with our Lord should strengthen our witness to the many who do not yet care to meet with us or with him; and the fact that so many may share the

Supper in peace should quicken our concern for those who have neither supper nor peace.

The sacrament of the Communion is a continual reminder of the cross of Christ.[21] It tells us that the cross is not really a thing of the past, but a present fact — that Christ is crucified afresh whenever sinful men act hatefully. It tells us that so long as sin is in the world crucifixion is the only way of life for those who would be after the order of the Son of God; and no one can partake of the Lord's Supper worthily who is not willing to carry his share of the load of the sin of mankind.

THE SPIRIT-GUIDED LIFE

The love of God is "richly poured," "unspent and free."[22] Nevertheless, there can be no fellowship between God and men who ignore the beckonings of his Spirit, and the responsibility which following him entails. To be pardoned by him we must extend pardon to others. This rule is fundamental, and cannot be waived for anyone. Jesus has stated this rule both positively and negatively:

> When ye stand praying, forgive if ye have aught against any; that your Father also who is in heaven, may forgive you your trespasses. But if you do not forgive, neither will your Father who is in heaven forgive your trespasses.[23]

This same requirement is made even more clear in one of the best known of our Lord's parables.[24] This parable is too long to quote in its entirety, but the point of this dramatic story lies in the comment made by Jesus regarding the debtor who had been forgiven large debts but who was unmerciful to a fellow servant who owed him a small debt. Jesus said:

> His lord was wroth, and delivered him to the tormentors, till he should pay all that was due unto him. So likewise shall my heavenly Father do also unto you, if ye from your hearts forgive not every one his brother their trespasses.

This obligation of mutual forgiveness rests most heavily on the body of those who profess his name, for if one who has borne the name of Christ should fall into sin, does not the possibility of his being restored to honor and decency depend very directly on the attitude of his fellows toward him? We dare not treat the sin of our fellowman lightly, yet if our judgment is merciless — if we seem to draw away from the pollution of his touch — may not our pitilessness hide the pity of God?[25] Here the church must take very seriously the task of representing Divinity. It is not too much to say that one of the major tasks confronting the church is to make the house of God the place where the cross of Christ is carried for the sake of sinners, and the witness that redemption is possible because the people of God bear one another's burdens.[26]

The problem of sin is the greatest problem confronting mankind. Yet "I am persuaded that neither death, nor life, . . . nor any other creature, shall be able to separate us from the love of God, which is in Christ Jesus our Lord."[27] It is in the light and the strength of this love, and of the assurance which he brings, that we seek harmony within and strive toward harmony without:

> Evil will remain with us as a problem until the day when Christian people are filled with the spirit of the cross of Christ. When "the love of Christ constraineth us," we shall find ourselves drawn into fellowship with God's eternal passion for overcoming evil with good. Then evil will not seem less evil, but more; and we shall view it with altered eyes. Now we look at sin, seeking to solve a problem; then we shall look at the sinful, seeking to save. Instead of a problem, we shall have a work; instead of a speculation, love; instead of pessimistic doubts, the hope that accompanies holy faith and high endeavor.[28]

---

1. Jer. 31:34; Heb. 8:12, 10:17.
2. Eph. 5:14-16; Col. 4:5.
3. Rev. 21:5.
4. John 14:26, 15:26, 16:7-15.

5. Acts 17:6.
6. II Cor. 10:4.
7. Acts 19:1-6.
8. Acts 8:15-17.
9. Acts 13:52.
10. Rom. 15:13.
11. I Pet. 1:8.
12. II Cor. 7:4; Heb. 10:34.
13. Matt. 26:22-24. See also Mark 14:20-23; Luke 22:19, 20.
14. I Cor. 11:27-29.
15. Eph. 4:16.
16. I Cor. 11:23.
17. John 6:53-58.
18. Matt. 5:25, 26.
19. D. and C. 46:1 d.
20. James 4:1-3.
21. I Cor. 10:16.
22. Samuel Johnson, *The Hymnal*, No. 296.
23. Mark 11:27, 28; see also Matt. 6:13.
24. Matt. 18:23-34.
25. H. R. McIntosh, *The Christian Experience of Forgiveness* (New York: Harper Brothers), p. 288.
26. Gal. 6:2.
27. Rom. 8:38, 39.
28. W. N. Clark, *The Christian Doctrine of God*, p. 462.

26 A Prophetic People

MAN by his own searching cannot find God;[1] consequently, down the ages, and out of his great love for mankind, God has therefore declared his nature and purpose through men of prophetic temper of mind. This has been so characteristic of the way of God with men that one of the prophets declared long ago: "Surely the Lord God will do nothing, until he revealeth the secret unto his servants the prophets."[2]

The prophets had a sense of intimate personal relationship with God. They felt that God had called them to his service and entrusted them with his word, a message of such preeminent importance that it must be proclaimed at any cost. They could not "prove" the truth of what they had to say, but they saw this truth vividly and felt it deeply as an artist sees and feels beauty. If their message was to be of any effect whatever, then the Spirit which inspired and sent them must bear witness to the heart and mind and conscience of their hearers.

The Ministry of the Prophets

The prophets were men of their times and knew those times. None of them spoke out of a vacuum, but each came to see the truth and the practical importance of his message in a familiar situation. Amos watched the fluctuation of grain prices as they were manipulated by wealthy men in a time of scarcity.[3]   Hosea had to contend with the sycophants in the royal court.[4]   Micah was himself a poor man who had first-hand experience of being cheated of the little he had earned.[5] Ezekiel was a captive among captives.[6] But they did not see these things as other men saw them.   Amos did not see the maneuvers of the grain market as an opportunity to make money, but as an instance of ungodly exploitation.   Hosea did not see the sycophancy of the royal favorites as a way to power, but as an evidence of moral decay.   Micah did not see the poverty of the poor as a fact of life to be accepted, but as an outrage against the justice for which God stands. Ezekiel's life was conditioned by his captivity, but led to his realization that God could be known in Babylon even as he had been known in Judea.[7]   This was because their ministry was rooted in a certainty of God, a certainty so fundamental that it permeated and gave meaning to all that they saw and thought and said and did.

People often consider the prophets in terms of foretelling or the revelation of future events; but there is little evidence that they were primarily concerned with this aspect of their ministry.   When they did foretell, this was incidental to their basic theme, a result of an illustration rather than an event in itself; but because the prophets were so deeply concerned about the truly significant happenings of their own times, they do speak to every generation of men, everywhere. And always their message is of the unmeasured splendor of God—his love, his justice, his mercy, his truth, and his anger against those who exploit the weak and oppress the poor and neglect the needy.   They saw God as the great Doer, an interested party in all that happens among men, one who is known by and through his mighty acts of judgment and deliverance.[8]

The prophets were preachers, many of whom delivered their word at great personal risk.   They denounced wickedness in biting terms which set forth its true character and left sinners without excuse. But they were not mere denunciators. They set forth a sound moral basis for life whenever they proclaimed man's absolute and inescapable obligation to God, his Creator. They had a contagious faith that, despite some-time appearances to the contrary, the divine purpose for man-kind is good. They taught that the strength of a community is in the fraternity and justice and truth to be found there. They gave life meaning and direction and purpose; and amid the disasters which overtook them and their people, they gave men a sense of basic security and a sound reason for hope.

Today, as always, we turn to the prophets in our repeatedly demonstrated need for spiritual insight. These insights cannot be won and made a permanent possession except as they are lived into reality, embodied in institutions and ways of life, and kept vital by the unceasing ministry of the Spirit of God. He who would fulfill the divine purpose in his life must learn for himself, in the practical situations of his daily life, the message of Hosea concerning the love of God, of Amos concerning social justice, of Jeremiah and Zephaniah concerning the judgment of God, and of Joseph Smith concerning the true nature of the kingdom of God.

THE GREATEST OF THE PROPHETS

The central conviction of the prophets was that the meaning of man's life lies in his relationship to God, and that our destiny is in the fulfillment of the purpose of God in our creation. This was the central conviction of the greatest of the prophets, the Lord Jesus Christ. His greatness is of a different order than that of the lesser prophets in that he fills in the meaning contained in their partial declarations. But, even more, his prophetic stature exceeds theirs, in that the word that he preached was embodied in his way of life and illustrated therein. In him, the word became flesh and dwelt among men.[9]

In the English language we are accustomed to contrast the terms "word" and "deed," but the Hebrews used a single term for both, because they expected a man to *do* what he *says*. With the Lord Jesus this was achieved to perfection. When he talked of purity, he meant the kind of purity which his disciples could see in his own life among them; when he talked of love, they knew that he meant such love as they had seen him show to those who hated him; when he talked of forgiveness, they remembered the forgiveness which he had extended to them after they denied him, and to the Romans when they crucified him. We do well to look back to the prophets for the inspired word, but we can only look to the Lord Jesus Christ for the completely inspired and inspiring life.

The moral greatness of the Lord Jesus Christ was not apparent to all who saw him, because only those who had caught something of his Spirit had the inner capacity required for understanding. To quote G. J. Chesterton, "A cat can look at a king, but a cat cannot *see* a king." The full glory of the love of God is shown in the fact that

> God, who at sundry times and in divers manners spake in times past unto the fathers by the prophets, hath in these last days spoken unto us by his Son.[10]

But it is brought to its fullness in that God has also given to men the Spirit by which they know that Jesus is indeed who he claims to be.[11]

By the Spirit of God we know that the Lord Jesus Christ is the answer to all our questions about God and about his purpose for our lives. This revelation will never be surpassed. Jesus is, as the early saints so joyously affirmed, "the same yesterday, today, and forever."[12] He is the best that any generation can imagine, and to be like him is the highest goal for all our striving; beyond him there are no excellencies for us to achieve.

A Prophetic People

When the children of Israel were on their way to the Promised Land, Moses found the burden of leadership too great for him and asked for relief. Soon after this, seventy of the elders were chosen to be associated with Moses, and at their consecration the Spirit of God rested upon them and they prophesied.[13] Meanwhile Eldad and Medad, who were of the seventy but who had remained with the people in the camp, also prophesied. When the news of Eldad and Medad was brought to Moses, Joshua was standing by and, jealous for the prophetic preeminence of his leader, he urged Moses to forbid further prophecy of this sort. In reply Moses set forth a principle which is fundamental to the life of the people of God. "Enviest thou for my sake?" he asked. "Would that all the Lord's people were prophets, and that the Lord would put his Spirit upon them."[14]

Many years later the prophet Joel set forth this principle in greater detail. Looking forward far beyond his own day he saw the coming of the time when men would seek the Lord with all their hearts and when the Spirit of God should be poured out upon "all flesh." He said, in the name of God,

> And it shall come to pass afterward, that I will pour out my Spirit upon all flesh; and your sons and your daughters shall prophesy, your old men shall dream dreams, your young men shall see visions; and also upon the servants and upon the handmaids in those days will I pour out my Spirit.[15]

On the day of Pentecost Peter recognized that the experience that he and the other disciples were then sharing was the partial fulfillment of the prophecy of Joel.[16] Again, at the beginning of the Restoration, the angel Moroni visited Joseph Smith and quoted this scripture to him,[17] explaining that it would be fulfilled in the near future. Beyond doubt, it is the will and purpose of God that his people shall be a prophetic people.

Although some men like Isaiah and Jeremiah and Joseph

Smith are specially chosen to be prophets, and are endowed to this end, there is a sense in which all those who come to know the truth of the prophetic word are themselves called to live by that word and to declare it. Even these never fully understand the nature and purpose of God. We who are of their number must be particularly careful not to regard our partial vision as complete and final. But if we are truly in the prophetic tradition, we are pointed in the right direction. We must still "follow on to know the Lord,"[18] and must keep "looking unto Jesus, the author and finisher of our faith."[19] But if we are faithful to this tradition, we will live in constant awareness of the rightful claims of God in the lives of men, and so we—as our daily lives provide recurring opportunities to learn to do according to the will of God on earth, as is done in heaven—will come to learn the grace of repentance on constantly higher levels.

THE MAKING OF A PROPHETIC PEOPLE

A recent prophetic message has reminded the church that the realization of the divine purpose among men is essentially a spiritual enterprise: "Zionic conditions are no further away nor any closer than the spiritual condition of my [God's] people justifies."[20]

What are the demands and the evidences of this "spiritual condition"? Quite evidently one of the characteristics required of the people of Zion is a high level of integrity such as was manifested by the prophets and is appropriate to a prophetic people. This integrity is of a special order. It is much more than the honesty of a good citizen. It is the pervasive unity of life and purpose which results from complete devotion to the highest that men can know. "If . . . thine eye be single," says the King James Version of the counsel of the Master, "thy whole body shall be full of light."[21] The Inspired Version makes this even clearer: "If . . . thine eye be single *to the glory of God,* thy whole body shall be full of

216

light." This is only possible in lives guided by the Spirit of God.

In light of what we have come to know, it also becomes evident that the work of God calls for the service of a mature people. This is not to say that the divine purpose cannot be served by a child or a childlike mind. We have the best of evidence that some of the characteristics of a little child are vital to the kingdom enterprise.[22] But the end to which new birth and Christian nurture point together is mature life and ministry such as draws on heart and soul and mind and strength.[23]

Again, spiritually mature people have emotional depth. The trend of modern life is frequently set against plumbing such depths. The modern man tries to escape deep involvement in the problems of life by taking refuge in his hobbies and by cultivating a so-called "peace of mind" which, at a time when moral issues are under attack, is often tantamount to a declaration of moral neutrality.

Consider the passionate concerns of Jesus. He never spoke a word of anger against people who mistreated him personally,[24] but only the blinding effect of our own shallowness as we think of the Master has dulled our appreciation of his anger at the vices, meannesses, dishonesties, and hypocrisies which he found among the religious people of his homeland.[25] Because he loved righteousness, he hated iniquity.[26] We never see Jesus truly until we see his capacity for sustained indignation against that which thwarted the purpose of his Father. After discussing the Master's indignation, Dr. Fosdick wrote:

> Here, then, are the marks of Jesus' indignation. He hated evil tremendously because he loved the people whom evil was ruining; his wrath was always unselfish, he was never angry at a private wrong; and his indignation always followed an attempt to find something praiseworthy in the man's life and was always ready to cease when the first sign of penitence appeared. Wrath like this explains the exclamation of a wise

217

Englishman: "Anger is one of the sinews of the soul; he who lacks it hath a maimed mind."[27]

Spiritual maturity requires that wisdom and love work hand in hand. The people of God should have neither time nor inclination to follow after every widely heralded cause which lays claim to their support. But, on the other hand, church members lack the maturity required of their calling if they stand supinely by while members of minority groups are exploited or are denied their human rights, or if they neglect their duties as citizens because they consider politics "dirty business," or if they manifest no sustained indignation against the betrayers of public trust, or make no significant protest when the children of the poor go hungry, or ill housed, or half educated. These are the things which have concerned the prophets, and the prophets have been concerned because it has been against such conditions that the wrath of God is kindled.

The spiritually mature man is aware of his own limitations and the limitations of his fellows. He does not think of himself more highly than he ought to think. But for that very reason he does his utmost to polish the gifts which God has given him, knowing that of its own nature love demands that his offering shall be the best that he can possibly give. His faith is too stalwart for him to refuse to inquire of learned men or to listen to them when they would teach him, and then to seek to justify his reticences because some have been shipwrecked when they set out, inadequately prepared, on voyages of intellectual discovery. He goes forward into life knowing that life calls us to many voyages, all of them hazardous, and that security lies, not in such treasuring of the fruits of the victories of yesterday as will leave unattempted the adventures which belong to our times but in a constant concern to know and to do the will of God.

There are other marks of a prophetic people, but they can all be gathered together under the concept of spiritual maturity. "God hath not given us the spirit of fear; but of

218

power and of love, and of a sound mind."[28] We are called to learn the difficult art of "speaking the truth in love" that in so doing we "may grow up into him in all things, which is the head, even Christ."[29]

The divine purpose in men can be fulfilled by a people of all-embracing integrity whose hearts turn to him in love, and whose minds and hands are set to the tasks which his prophet-messengers have shown to be of unfailing importance. There is no other way in which the divine purpose in man can be achieved.

1. Job 11:7.
2. Amos 3:7.
3. Amos 8:4, 5.
4. Hosea 7:3, 5.
5. Micah 2:1, 2; 3:1-3 ff.
6. Ezekiel 1:1.
7. Discussed in *Ground to Stand On*, John H. Otwell, Oxford University Press, p. 186.
8. Isaiah 28:21.
9. John 1:14.
10. Heb. 1:1, 2.
11. Matt. 16:18.
12. Heb. 13:8.
13. Num. 11:25.
14. Num. 11:29.
15. Joel 2:28, 29.
16. Acts 2:17, 18.
17. *Church History*, Vol. 1, p. 14.
18. Hosea 6:3.
19. Heb. 12:2.
20. D. and C. 140:5 c.
21. Matt. 6:22.
22. Matt. 18:2-5.
23. Mark 12:30, K.J.; Mark 12:35, I.V.
24. I Pet. 2:23.
25. Matt. 23:23-28; Mark 3:5; Luke 13:32, 17:2; John 2:13-17.
26. Heb. 1:9.
27. Harry Emerson Fosdick, *The Manhood of the Master* (New York: Association Press, 1958), p. 45.
28. II Tim. 1:7.
29. Eph. 4:15.

27 | The Christian Hope

FOURTEEN centuries before Columbus set sail, the apostle Paul also started on a voyage, and this voyage was as significant for our spiritual life as the voyage of Columbus was for our physical progress.[1] Columbus sailed to discover the new world. He made his journey out of his conviction regarding the nature of the physical universe. Paul sailed, a prisoner, to make the old world new. He made his journey out of his conviction regarding the nature of the Eternal God.

Journeys by sea were fraught with adventure in the days of Paul, and his journey was no exception. The ship on which he was traveling was caught in a storm somewhere in the Adriatic Sea, and for fourteen days the passengers and crew were in constant danger of death. They lowered the sails and jettisoned the cargo and abandoned the ship's gear, but none of these measures met their desperate situation. Then, when all hope seemed lost, Paul took command, relying less on his seamanship or his native ingenuity than on the promises which God had made to him. His faith and hope proved the salvation of everyone aboard.

The hope which enabled Paul to save himself and his shipmates was peculiar to him and his situation; but it was related to a larger hope which is characteristic of the people of God—a hope which is born of the spirit's grip on ultimate realities, and which is the motive power by which the man of God lives from day to day as he faces confidently the seemingly insurmountable moral and spiritual and practical obstacles which confront him.

Let us now consider the Christian hope in terms of its bearing on the achievement of the divine purpose in us.

HOPE FACES FACTS

The Christian hope faces frankly the major enemies of mankind, sin and death. It acknowledges that we have taken the precious gift of freedom and made it the instrument of our selfishness, that this willful way of life has become characteristic of our entire race, that modern progress has done nothing to cure this fatal weakness, and that there is no hope for man in man. It acknowledges, also, that death comes to all of us at the time of its own choosing; but it also affirms that both of these dread evils have been met and overcome, and Christian hope is built on this confrontation and this victory.

Men of God look forward in confidence born of the great acts of God in the past, and find in them ground for hope for what is yet to be. In the final analysis this hope is built on the nature of God himself. The Psalmist wrote, "Happy is he . . . whose hope is in the Lord,"[2] and Jeremiah declared, "Blessed is the man . . . whose hope the Lord is."[3] But the full and sound hope of the Saints finds its best support in the fact that God raised Jesus from the dead after wicked men had done the worst that they could do to him. Ever since the morning of the first Easter men of spiritual discernment have known that the last word rests with God and not with men. So the apostle Paul could write:

> We are troubled on every side, yet not distressed; we are perplexed, but not in despair; persecuted, but not forsaken; cast down, but not destroyed.[4]

And Peter could be sure of their understanding when he wrote to his fellow Christians:

> Blessed be the God and Father of our Lord Jesus Christ, which according to his abundant mercy hath begotten us again unto a lively hope by the resurrection of Jesus Christ from the dead.[5]

For those who do not know Christ in the power of his resurrection, death is the limit of all endeavor. Even if they find comfort in the thought that they will someday "join the choir invisible of those immortal dead who live again in minds made better by their presence,"[6] this but postpones the victory of death. But in Christ the whole situation is changed. He sets new boundaries to our existence and does so in such a way as to change the significance of all that has gone before. In the light of the resurrection we can commit ourselves and all our concerns into his hands with complete confidence, knowing that sin and death have been robbed of their power and that in him and through him we are "more than conquerors."

With such a foundation, hope amid tribulation was characteristic of the New Testament saints. Their hope was not just an added virtue among others; it was a dominant note in their lives, marking the difference between the Christians and the non-Christians. To quote Dr. T. R. Glover, "the Christians out-thought, and out-hoped, and out-lived, and out-died the pagans." They rejoiced in their coming victory with a conviction which grew out of their faith in the God and Father of our Lord Jesus Christ. They sang songs at midnight even though they were fastened in the stocks. They made of their martyrdom an act of worship, even though they died in agony in the amphitheater or in the gardens of Nero.

Something like this has been true of men of faith all down the years. When Rome was sacked by the invading barbarians, and the power which had made the world one world was about to be disintegrated, it was then that Augustine wrote his vision of the City of God. It was when his world was torn with dissension, and he himself was in Bedford jail that John Bunyan wrote his story of the *Pilgrim's Progress*. It was when Bishop Butler refused to become Archbishop of Canterbury because he said that it was too late to save a dying church, that the Wesleys and Whitfields were winning common people to Christ in the greatest revival of the century, a revival that saved England from the horrors of revolution which embroiled her neighbor across the channel. All these, and many thousands more, who have wrought mightily in the name of Christ, have done so because of the hope within them. This hope did not reflect a superficial response to the circumstances of their times, but was an outgrowth of their experience with God in Christ. Again and again it seemed to be totally incompatible with the only facts which other men thought significant, and yet again and again it proved to be the key to victory. It was not because Paul despised human wisdom and prudence, but because he knew that these must serve and not seek to replace the loving wisdom and counsel of God, that the apostle declared:

> We preach Christ crucified, unto the Jews a stumbling-block, and unto the Greeks foolishness; but unto them who believe, both Jews and Greeks, Christ the power of God, and the wisdom of God. . . . The foolishness of God is wiser than men; and the weakness of God is stronger than men. . . . Not many wise men after the flesh, not many mighty, not many noble, are chosen; for God hath chosen the foolish things of the world to confound the wise; and God hath chosen the weak things of the world to confound the things which are mighty; and base things of the world, and things which are despised, hath God chosen, yea, and things which are not, to bring to naught things that are mighty; that no flesh should glory in his presence. But of him are ye in Christ Jesus, who of God is made unto us wisdom, and righteousness, and sanctification, and redemption; that, according as it is written, He that glorieth, let him glory in the Lord.[7]

THY WILL BE DONE

We have already seen that even our noblest purposes fall short of the purpose God has set for us in the life of Christ and in the ministry of the Holy Spirit. Our human contrivances and our scientific knowledge are always in part wrongly directed. For this reason we dare not confine our hopes for tomorrow to what we can now anticipate. We have a sure foundation for hope, but this hope is in God and not in ourselves. It is not in having our own way, but in God who has his loving way in us. The Christian hope is misunderstood except as we see that its deepest characteristic is to trust God's sovereign love for us without counseling him as to where that love shall lead.

The life of hope is a life of high level achievement in love. It is not a hope to avoid responsibility and suffering, for these are of the warp and woof of life. In the long run they can only be avoided by sacrificing something which belongs to life itself. Rather, the Christian hope is the well-grounded assurance that "by patient continuance in well doing," as God shall give us power to see and to do, we shall come at last to immortality and eternal life in the fellowship of the faithful, and that all the sacrifice and endurance of the past shall be found to be part of our victory.

The Christian hope of the future does not depend on any perfection of our outward circumstances, but on the enrichment of our inner life. We cannot imagine what that future will be like, for our imagination is rooted in what has been, and old scenes are changing at a dizzying pace. But we do not need to know these details. We do know that Christ is Lord of the future, "the same yesterday, today, and forever," and this invites and encourages us to prepare to play our part with him in his coming day.

> Behold, what manner of love the Father hath bestowed upon us that we should be called the sons of God; therefore the world knoweth us not, because it knew him not. Beloved, now are we the sons of God, and it doth not yet appear what we shall be; but we know that, when he shall appear, we shall be like him; for we shall see him as he is. And every man that hath this hope in him purifieth himself, even as he is pure.[8]

Medieval Christian thinkers used to list the deadly sins. In view of the resources of the Saints, despair certainly belongs in such a list, for the hopeless man has closed his heart and his mind to the great and precious promises which form a great part of the good news of the gospel. He has lost faith in the divine will or the divine power to bring men through to victory. Scaling down his expectations, he sees no meaning to life and therefore no hope for the future. And when this happens, morality goes with the hopelessness which his loss breeds.

In days when life seems to be dominated by hatred and fear, when the genius of so many is dedicated to destruction, and when the mass movements of mankind seem to make individual effort futile, it is of earth-shaking importance that we shall hold high our hope in Christ. Despite all appearances to the contrary, God is still the Lord of life. His "exceeding great and precious promises" are grounded in his very nature. His good purpose toward us will not be denied. None can pluck out of his hand those who put their trust in him, and live under his guidance:

> If we shall endure, we shall be kept according to his promise. And we look for a new heavens, and a new earth wherein dwelleth righteousness. Wherefore, beloved, seeing that ye look for such things, be diligent, that ye may be found of him in peace, without spot and blameless.[9]

---

1. Acts 27.
2. Ps. 146:5.
3. Jer. 17:7.
4. II Cor. 4:8, 9.
5. I Peter 1:3.
6. George Eliot.
7. I Cor. 1:23-31.
8. I John 3:1-3.
9. II Peter 3:13, 14.

Questions and Discussion Topics

PREFACE

I suggest that those who are to teach classes use the suggestions in this section as guides in preparing for class presentations and discussions.

The questions and discussion topics are merely suggestive. No teacher should feel that he is required to use them, or to be confined to them.

Questions and discussions will be more fruitful if they arise in the course of the lesson and are, in fact, the work of the teacher even though they may be phrased in the words which are here suggested. It is simply not possible to prepare questions that fit every situation, and the teacher's function, among others, is to see that the class discussions are directed to the needs and interests of his particular class. This means that the questions which are appropriate to another group which is studying this book may not be appropriate to your group as you study it.

In my own teaching I have found it helpful to make a two- or three-minute summary at the end of a class period rather than to leave the discussion up in the air. You may want to do this. You may also find it profitable in such a summary to relate the understanding achieved in the class to our basic concern, the divine purpose in us.

Proceed at your own pace. There is no law which says you have to cover a chapter in a week.

God bless you in your ministry.

F. HENRY EDWARDS

WHAT IS MAN?

Lesson 1

(Chapter 1, pp. 10-15)

LESSON PURPOSE

To consider both the grandeur and the dependence of man, and to contrast the importance of the "inward man" and the "outward man"

POINTS TO KEEP IN MIND

Man's greatness reflects the greatness of his Creator.

To be in the image of God indicates potential even more than endowment.

Man is rich but dependent, and there is no escape from this dependence.

God and man belong together.

QUESTIONS AND DISCUSSION TOPICS

1. In what sense is it true that man is the noblest of the animals? Is this all the truth about the nature of man? In what sense can we rightly say that an animal is "noble"?

2. What did the prophets mean when they taught that man is created in the image of God? What do you mean when you use this expression?

3. Name some human characteristics not shared by the animals. To what part of man's life do these belong?

4. Give illustrations of the expanding dominion of mankind. What is the significance of this growing power? Can it mislead us? How?

5. The text states that "the stupendously significant fact of the universe is that man is, and that we are on the way to greatness." Do you agree? If so, name the guarantees that this is so.

6. An ancient proverb says, "He that is slow to anger is better than the mighty; and he that ruleth his spirit than he that taketh a city" (Prov. 16:32). Discuss this in the light of the chapter under review. If a doubter questioned this, how would you support it?

7. Why do we need "a new heart and a new spirit"? Give illustrations supporting your answer.

8. Do you agree that "our very greatness brings us to the point of desperate need"? Why is this so? Is our need likely to become more urgent or less so?

229

9. Discuss man's dependence and his independence with a view to seeing clearly how far each of these is justified.
10. Paul says that "though our outward man perish, yet the inward man is renewed day by day" (II Cor. 4:16). Under what conditions is this true? Does this mean that we should despise our "outward man"?
11. What major conclusions have you drawn from considering the nature of man?

LIFE IS PURPOSEFUL

Lesson 2

(Chapter 2, pp. 16-23)

LESSON PURPOSE

To emphasize the importance of an adequate life purpose

POINTS TO KEEP IN MIND

The key to understanding the greatness of the Hebrew people is in their sense of destiny under God.

The basic affirmations concerning God and man found in the book of Genesis are true for all time.

These all point to the importance of a life purpose centered in God who is our Creator.

QUESTIONS AND DISCUSSION TOPICS

1. How do you account for the impact of the Hebrew people on the course of history?
2. Consider the major affirmations of the book of Genesis listed in this chapter. Have they ever been outmoded? What is their significance in relation to our life purpose?
3. What is the difference between progress and movement? What is the connection between the idea of progress and the idea of purpose?
4. Science traces cause and effect. It does not affirm purpose. How may religion help science at this point?
5. How does a controlling purpose release power for life? Illustrate your answer, both affirmatively and negatively.
6. Discuss the effect of comparatively exclusive devotion to a small life purpose. In what way does fervent devotion to a great cause make for greatness?

7. In what way has your faith affected your life purpose? What has been its effect on the secondary purposes of your life?

8. Consider persons you know who have a consistent life purpose and who follow it without undue strain. What lessons do they have for us?

9. Contrast your life purpose of a few years ago and your present life purpose. In what ways has your purpose changed? Why? Do you expect further changes? In what direction will these changes be pointed? Why?

10. Under what circumstances can you best evaluate the nature and quality of your own life purposes?

THE GLORY OF GOD

Lesson 3

(Chapter 3, pp. 24-30)

LESSON PURPOSE

To affirm and justify the Christian conviction that the reason for our existence is the fulfillment of the purpose of God in our creation

POINTS TO KEEP IN MIND

There is sound reason for our existence, or all life is unreasonable.

The reason affirmed by Christianity unites all creation under God.

We perceive the divine purpose in us most convincingly and most creatively in experiences of worship, when the vision of the moment is uplifted by awareness of the majesty of God, our Father.

QUESTIONS AND DISCUSSION TOPICS

1. Men are created beings. What is the significance of this fact in relation to a sound life purpose for man?

2. The church affirms that Christ Jesus our Lord was the active agent in all creation. Discuss the significance of this belief in terms of (1) our life purpose and (2) what it teaches about the unity of creation.

3. Discuss man's dependence and independence. Where does one end and the other begin?

231

4. If we are so fully dependent on God, how can we be held responsible for fulfillment of his purpose in us?
5. Discuss the statement in this chapter that "Man's freedom is for God and in God, not against God."
6. It has been said that our greatest glory is to share the work of creation with God. What part do we have in creation? Consider this against the background of the development of maturity in a good family.
7. Discuss the contribution made by genuine worship to the understanding of our life purpose and to our glad acceptance of this purpose as the best possible one for us.
8. What is the effect of becoming gratefully convinced that God has a plan for our lives?
9. How can we best extol the glory of God? Why should we do so? How does the love of God minister to the fulfillment of his purpose in us?

THE PURPOSE OF LIFE REVEALED IN JESUS CHRIST

Lesson 4

(Chapter 4, pp. 31-35)

LESSON PURPOSE

To present the Lord Jesus Christ as the perfect example of life lived according to the divine purpose.

POINTS TO EMPHASIZE

Jesus Christ is the essential clue to the meaning of life.
Only the Son of God can fully reveal God.
Only a perfect man can reveal the nature of man.
Christian faith is directly opposed to any scheme of self-redemption.

QUESTIONS AND DISCUSSION TOPICS

1. Do you believe that Jesus was truly human? Was he "a true man" in a finer sense than any other man?
2. What reason do you have for the faith of the church that Jesus is truly and fully divine?
3. What is the meaning of the apostolic statement that the Lord Jesus Christ is "the brightness of his [Father's] glory, and the express image of his person"?

4. State various ways in which God is revealed, illustrating each of them.
5. Do you agree that only the Son of God can fully reveal his Father? Justify your answer.
6. John promises that "we shall see him [Jesus] as he is." What capacities for understanding must be developed in us before this will be possible?
7. Discuss the meaning of the statement that the Lord Jesus Christ is our "elder brother." What light does this throw on the possibilities of human nature?
8. What do we mean when we say that Jesus is our great example? Must we copy him in the minutiae of life? If not, where do we draw the line?
9. Why is it impossible for men to save themselves? What does the Lord Jesus do for us that we cannot do for ourselves?
10. What contribution does the Lord Jesus make to our understanding of the purpose of God in us?

OUR PURPOSE AND THE HOLY SPIRIT

Lesson 5

(Chapter 5, pp. 36-43)

LESSON PURPOSE

To show that God seeks to confirm his purpose in us by the creative inner ministries of his Holy Spirit

POINTS TO EMPHASIZE

There is a purpose in history higher than man himself has been able to supply.

God can bring his purpose to pass without violating human agency, and does so.

The Holy Spirit continues the work of Christ. This is essentially a ministry of persuasion.

QUESTIONS AND DISCUSSION TOPICS

1. The text states that "Usually the hand of God is unobtrusive." Do you agree? Why should this be so?
2. How may the gifts of ungodly men promote the advance of the race? What does this mean in terms of human agency?

3. Do you agree that the "prophets and seers have been among the most significant figures in the march of men toward the heights"? Give reasons for your answer.

4. Discuss ways in which proper response to the duties and obligations of daily life minister to the fulfillment of the divine purpose in us.

5. What is the relation between the work of the Lord Jesus Christ and the work of the Holy Spirit? Can we understand one without the other? Discuss your answer.

6. Distinguish between facts and truth. What truths are the primary concern of the Holy Spirit?

7. How can beauty lead us to an appreciation of the purpose of God in our lives? Can the pursuit of beauty become an end in itself? If so, is this an illustration of the second best becoming the enemy of the best? Discuss this, including ways in which this threat can be avoided.

8. Name some of your own heroes in the struggle for righteousness. What outstanding value does each of them stand for? Are these values sufficient of themselves?

9. How does the Holy Spirit minister to our achievement of the purpose of God in us? Is this ministry personal or social?

10. Do you believe that an ungodly man lives a narrow and restricted life? To what degree is this because he does not see the true meaning and purpose of life? How may the Holy Spirit enlighten him in these matters? Is the Spirit likely to operate directly, or through the lives of those who are already Spirit-guided? What does this mean in terms of responsibility of those who are blessed by the ministry of the Spirit?

THE CHURCH AND THE PURPOSE OF LIFE

Lesson 6

(Chapter 6, pp. 44-49)

LESSON PURPOSE

To make clear and impressive the place held by the church in enabling us to see and achieve the purpose of God in our lives

Points to Emphasize

To be a disciple of Christ is to be a member of his body.
The church was formed to continue the work of Jesus Christ in
   the world under the direction of the Holy Spirit.
The church needs our special talents and supplies our lacks.
The church unites the generations.

Questions and Discussion Topics

1. Discuss and illustrate the statement that "A man is truly
   himself only insofar as he has interests and investments in
   other people."

2. Discuss the statement that "Spiritual life is based on spiritual
   fellowship." Why does the New Testament show no interest in unattached Christians?

3. What are the evidences that the church is "a divine creation
   rather than a human institution"?

4. Cite some scriptural evidences showing the importance of
   the church in the divine plan.

5. How do past generations enrich the worship life of the
   church? How do they enable us to see more clearly the
   divine purpose in us? How do they depend on us for their
   fulfillment?

6. Consider the function of the church in saving us from self-
   centeredness, from parochialism, from chauvinism, and other
   "isms."

7. What are the central functions of the church which cannot
   be met by any other organization?

8. Discuss the types of opportunity for spiritual development
   found in the church, the dependence of the church on the
   contributions of its members, and ways in which church
   members fail to derive from the church the strength and
   guidance which they need.

9. What do we mean by the expression "the tradition of the
   elders"? Of what value is this tradition? What are the
   dangers of following this tradition too closely? How may
   we be safeguarded from such dangers?

10. How has the church enriched your understanding of the
    divine purpose in your life, and your attitude toward this
    divine purpose?

THE SPIRIT AND THE BODY

(Chapter 7, pp. 50-55)

LESSON PURPOSE

To make clear the relation of the body and spirit; to emphasize the spiritual importance of our present opportunities

POINTS TO EMPHASIZE

There is need for balanced understanding of the relation of body and spirit.

The purpose of God for men includes the redemption of our material existence.

Knowledge of the divine purpose is enhanced and made fruitful as skills are cultivated and dedicated.

The spirit and the body is the soul of man.

QUESTIONS AND DISCUSSION TOPICS

1. What are the two major temptations of Christianity in regard to the spirit and the body? Name some ways in which the first of these is frequently expressed. Name some ways in which the second of them is frequently expressed.

2. How has the Lord Jesus Christ helped us to see the importance of material things? What do we mean by "the sacramental nature of our bodily life"? Cite evidences that the spirit depends upon matter as its means of expression. Can you think of any contrary indication? Does this mean that a man cannot rise above his physical limitations? Discuss this.

3. When we refer to "the body" in contrast with "the spirit," what does this include?

4. Discuss pride in good workmanship. Is it good or bad? How can it be made good? Can we honestly offer poor workmanship as our contribution to human well-being?

5. Discuss the scriptural doctrine that our earthly life is a time of probation. What is its purpose? In this connection discuss the meaning of the statement that "Not until the truth is embodied in life, and illuminated thereby, is it really ours."

6. What is the divinely approved relation between faith and understanding? Why do I not have any right to be the sole beneficiary of the product of my skills?

7. List the major characteristics of the most spiritual men you know. Exchange them with other members of the group. What do we mean when we say that a man is spiritual?
8. Modern revelation says that the spirit and the body is the soul of man. Discuss the truth and the importance of this statement.

HIGHER LEVELS OF LIFE

Lesson 8

(Chapter 8, pp. 56-64)

LESSON PURPOSE

To recognize the rightful place in the divine scheme of things of such matters as pleasure and comfort and success and their relative unimportance as compared with basic character

POINTS TO EMPHASIZE

The New Testament shows concern for life on a high level.
There is positive joy in spiritual achievement.
There is security of joy on the higher levels.
Salvation is not freedom from sorrow, but from sin.

QUESTIONS AND DISCUSSION TOPICS

1. What did Paul mean when he wrote that "To be carnally minded is death; but to be spiritually minded is life and peace"? Do you agree? Illustrate your answer if possible.
2. Under what circumstances is "the pursuit of happiness" in conflict with the achievement of the divine purpose in us? Discuss the importance of challenging tasks.
3. Why cannot lasting comfort be found in the pursuit of pleasure or comfort? Illustrate your answer.
4. Distinguish between "pleasure" and "joy." What is the meaning of the statement that "Men are, that they might have joy"?
5. What is the foundation of abiding joy? Name some who have possessed such joy. How did they get it?
6. Consider George Matheson's hymn, "O Love That Wilt Not Let Me Go." Discuss the meaning of the "joy that seekest me through pain," and the "cross that liftest up my head."

7. Name some virtues which should be cultivated at all costs. Are we likely to seek these virtues persistently if life has no larger meaning than is apparent to the man without faith?
8. Discuss possible definitions for success. Are there any areas in which we can command success? What are they? What is it to be saved, in terms of the discussion of this chapter?

PURPOSE AND IMMORTALITY

Lesson 9

(Chapter 9, pp. 65-71)

LESSON PURPOSE

To consider the divine purpose in the light of immortality

POINTS TO EMPHASIZE

Against the background of eternity, death is a friend.
God is the final evidence for immortality.
Immortality is needed to give scope to the finest of our present expectations.
We must live now in the light of eternity.

QUESTIONS AND DISCUSSION TOPICS

1. In what sense is death a friend, and in what sense an enemy? What aspects of life does death clearly terminate? What does this indicate concerning these aspects of life?
2. How does death add meaning to life?
3. In what sense do we know that we are immortal? In what sense is our conviction of immortality an affirmation of faith?
4. List some of the evidences of immortality. Which of these do you consider the greatest? May other evidences be said to derive from this one?
5. Discuss the statement of the text that "We need eternity in which to complete the vision of the hour." Give illustrations of this truth.
6. Paul wrote, "And now abideth faith, hope, charity." In what way does each of these abiding realities deny the finality of death?

238

7. How does the hope of immortality affect present moral standards?
8. How may we best prepare for the life hereafter? Does such preparation enrich or impoverish our present life?
9. How does consideration of immortality enrich our understanding of the divine purpose in us?

PURPOSE AND ETERNAL LIFE

Lesson 10

(Chapter 10, pp. 72-78)

LESSON PURPOSE

To see and appreciate those present values which truly ought to be secure from the threat of death, and which enter into the divine purpose for us

POINTS TO EMPHASIZE

Eternal life is a life of the Father, and of the Son, and of the Holy Spirit.

We can share this life now.

It is most clearly perceived in the acts of worship.

It is a life of seeking and response to the highest.

QUESTIONS AND DISCUSSION TOPICS

1. Distinguish between immortality and eternal life. How are they related, and how are they separate from each other?
2. Discuss the meaning of Paul's expressions "carnally minded" and "spiritually minded."
3. How does personal worship enrich our understanding of eternal life? What contributions may be made by the study of great literature? of the scriptures?
4. What additional insights are given us in corporate worship? What is the pervasive spirit of effective corporate worship?
5. Discuss eternal life as the life of God in the soul of man.
6. In what sense is eternal life the life of obedience and of submission? How can it also be the life of freedom?
7. Eternal life is not something given as a reward, but is the life of God developed in us as we grow more and more like him. If this is so, how is eternal life related to other aspects of life?

8. The text states that eternal life is "the life of grace." What does this mean? How is this different from life lived in obedience to the law?
9. When does eternal life begin? How does it begin? What do you find to be its major enemies?
10. In what sense can we earn eternal life? In what sense is it the gift of God? In what sense is it the fulfillment of the divine purpose in us?

OUR PURPOSE REVEALED IN THE KINGDOM

Lesson 11

(Chapter 11, pp. 79-87)

LESSON PURPOSE

To study the nature of the kingdom of God so as to see that here the divine purpose is progressively achieved

POINTS TO EMPHASIZE

Our urgent need is for a moral and spiritual revolution.

The kingdom is not the perfection of human endeavor. It can only be achieved by reborn men, under God.

It is a highly demanding gift.

Devotion to the cause of Christ and his kingdom is the way of salvation.

QUESTIONS AND DISCUSSION TOPICS

1. Do you agree that civilization is now at the crossroads? Cite some evidences of the need for a searching moral and spiritual revolution.
2. Why must the coming of the kingdom be heralded by individual conversion? What are the major evidences that an individual has been truly converted?
3. What are the distinctions between the kingdom of God and the kingdoms of men? In what sense is the kingdom of God the fulfillment of the hope of the ages? How many does it require in order to build the kingdom?
4. What truths about the kingdom are taught in the parables of the leaven, the hidden treasure, the pearl of great price, the growing seed, the ten virgins?

5. In what sense is the kingdom of God the gift of God? In what sense is this gift an achievement? Is there any necessary conflict between the two? Illustrate your answers.

6. How does the kingdom grow? How may we add to this growth, and quicken it?

7. What do we mean when we describe the kingdom as "the kingdom of brotherly love"? Is this an emotional achievement? Is that all?

8. "We do not know what the kingdom of God is like, only the direction in which it is to be found." Discuss the truth sought to be expressed here. What are the abiding aspects of the kingdom, carrying over from our present life?

9. How does the concept of the kingdom enrich our understanding of the divine purpose in us?

THE UNFOLDING PURPOSE

Lesson 12, Part I Review

(Chapters 1-11)

LESSON PURPOSE

To review the major emphases of the preceding lessons, noting that the purpose of God in us becomes constantly clearer as we are responsive to it

METHOD

Selected topics from the following list may be assigned to members of the class sometime in advance of the review, with the instructions that they be prepared to lead brief discussions in these fields.

Or it may be preferred to take a cross section of what has been discussed and approach this in similar fashion.

DISCUSSION TOPICS

The importance of a life purpose

Why the purpose of God is the best purpose for man

How the purpose of life is revealed in the life of the Lord Jesus Christ

How the purpose of life is clarified in us by the ministry of the Holy Spirit

The contribution of the church to our understanding of the true
purpose of life
The importance of daily tasks in fulfilling the purpose of life
The scriptural meaning of "life"
The light thrown on the purpose of life by the fact of immortality
The purpose of God and eternal life
The achievement of the purpose of life in the building of the
kingdom of God

ALTERNATE DISCUSSION TOPICS

The nature of an adequate purpose for human life
Man's inescapable need of God
Man's need of an adequate pattern for life
Spiritual guidance and the fulfillment of the purpose of life
Spiritual resources of the community of believers
The importance of the daily task in seeing and fulfilling the
purpose of life
The Christian attitude toward pain, sorrow, and failure
The meaning of eternal life
Fulfilling the purpose of life in building the kingdom of God

THE NATURE OF OUR FREEDOM

Lesson 13

(Chapter 12, pp. 90-97)

LESSON PURPOSE

To make clear the nature of human freedom, its limitations and
responsibilities

POINTS TO EMPHASIZE

That freedom is necessarily limited
The social, intellectual, and spiritual factors in freedom
The reality of human freedom
Freedom and responsibility

QUESTIONS AND DISCUSSION TOPICS

1. Discuss the meaning of the statement: When you choose a
course of action, you choose its consequences.

2. Do you agree that men of intemperate minds are not free? Explain your answer. Discuss what light this throws on the nature of freedom.
3. How is freedom limited by past choices? What significance should this have in the life program of a wise man?
4. Name other ways in which human freedom is limited.
5. Give reasons for believing that men are truly free. What would happen if we did not believe in such freedom?
6. In what way does commitment to a cause make for freedom? Is it possible to achieve greater freedom by giving up some rights?
7. Note the meaning of predestination as set forth in the text and discuss its relation to freedom.
8. What is the meaning of the statement that man is "an agent unto himself"? In what sense does this mean that he is responsible to God?
9. Discuss the relationship of responsibility and freedom. What is the responsibility of free men with regard to the freedom of other men?
10. Discuss the meaning of freedom in light of this chapter. How is it related to the divine purpose in man?

AGENCY AND SIN

Lesson 14

(Chapter 13, pp. 98-108)

LESSON PURPOSE

To present sin as rebellion and to emphasize the need to be clear-eyed about sin if we are to fulfill the divine purpose in us

POINTS TO EMPHASIZE

The meaning of human freedom is determined by the fact that man is a created being.

We cannot know the nature and extent of our sinfulness without such a standard as the Lord Jesus Christ.

Without agency there is no responsibility, and without responsibility there is no sin.

Sin is godlessness: an attitude more than a specific act.

243

1. Name some of the evidences that man tends to think and act as though he were God.

2. Do you believe that many men are too complacent about sin? Can we be too concerned about sin? In what sense is sin the root cause of human bondage?

3. In what ways does the Lord Jesus Christ help us to see our own sinfulness? Is this a service to us, or would it be better if we were left undisturbed? Give reasons for your answers.

4. List some factors which need to be kept in mind as we work toward the definition of sin. Note the relation between sin and error and between sin and ignorance. Discuss sin as selfishness and as rebellion.

5. Are evil thoughts truly sinful? Distinguish between temptation and sins. Would you agree that *entertaining* sinful thoughts is the significant factor here?

6. Discuss the relation between sin and agency.

7. Is it likely that we shall ever escape temptation in this life?

8. Discuss the statement, "All men sin, but men are not merely sinners."

ORIGINAL SIN

Lesson 15

(Chapter 14, pp. 109-116)

LESSON PURPOSE

To appreciate more clearly the social significance of sin and the responsibility of individuals for the social consequences of their sinning.

POINTS TO EMPHASIZE

Our way of life contrary to the divine purpose
The truth embodied in the doctrine of the Fall
The truth sought to be conveyed in the doctrine of original sin
The reality of redemption

QUESTIONS AND DISCUSSION TOPICS

1. Do you agree that "we come into the world with a definite tendency to choose some evil"? Is the reverse of this also true? Discuss.

2. What is meant by the doctrine of total depravity? Give reasons for believing or refusing to believe in this doctrine.

3. What are the essential truths expressed in the doctrine of the Fall?

4. Discuss the relation of self-assertion to the development of one's own powers. What bearing does the attitude of wise and loving parents have on this point? Is the necessity for self-assertion related to the amount of wisdom and love available? Suppose that these were infinite, what effect would this have on the necessity for self-assertion?

5. Distinguish between manliness and godliness. Consider whether you would describe Jesus Christ as a "manly man." Is your point of view here influenced by your limited idea of what it is to be manly?

6. Discuss briefly the statement that "The sins of the fathers are visited on the children to the third and fourth generation." Is this just? Is it avoidable?

7. How would you explain the difference between "original sin" and "original guilt"?

8. How fully is it true that we are each responsible for the social consequences of our acts? What does avoidance of responsibility for the moral tone of his generation do to the inner quality of a man?

9. Discuss ways in which the social solidarity of the generations has strengthened man in his fight against sin.

10. Does repentance free us of social responsibility for sin? What guidance does the life and death of the Lord Jesus Christ have for us at this point?

11. Discuss the meaning of stewardship in the light of the lessons in this chapter.

12. Discuss the need for the redemption of the entire social order in light of the insights of this chapter.

YOUR SIN AND MINE

Lesson 16

(Chapter 15, pp. 117-126)

LESSON PURPOSE

To face together the responsibility of the people of God in view of the social forces which are sinful and which lead men into sin.

POINTS TO EMPHASIZE

Sin is never seen truly except against the background of the love of God.

Our good intentions can blind us to our involvement in sinful ways of life.

No man can divorce himself from some measure of responsibility for the sins of society.

The first step toward our redemption is to face the fact of our sinfulness as this is revealed in the life and ministry of Jesus Christ.

QUESTIONS AND DISCUSSION TOPICS

1. Discuss the statement that "The characteristic work of sin in most of us is to blind us to the sinfulness of our sinning."
2. Discuss ways in which the worst enemy of the best may be the second best.
3. Comment on ways in which the types of sins listed in the chapter are violations of the commandment to love God.
4. Can a man be truly honest who appropriates his natural gifts to his own purposes?
5. Why do you feel that obligations go with the gifts of God? Is this sense of obligation a human achievement or is it also a gift of God?
6. What is the meaning of hypocrisy? Who are most likely to be susceptible to the temptations of hypocrisy?
7. What social sins do you find especially hateful? What should the church do about them?
8. What should be the attitude of church members toward such organizations as Alcoholics Anonymous? Discuss the balance between rightful involvement and radical commitment to crusades for social righteousness.
9. How did Jesus promote social righteousness?

246

10. What do we mean by "besetting sins"? What are the besetting sins of the Saints? How may we help each other
to see these sins without provoking a self-defeating resentment?
11. Discuss the significance of the statement that Jesus "breaks
the power of cancelled sin." What power does cancelled
sin have?
12. What do you consider the major resources available in the
fight against wickedness in high places?

AGENCY IN THE MODERN WORLD

Lesson 17

(Chapter 16, pp. 127-135)

LESSON PURPOSE

To cultivate a sense of responsibility for insights and actions
appropriate to our modern world

POINTS TO EMPHASIZE

The personal aspects of life are its most important concerns.
The modern world confronts us with special demands for wise
and morally sound action.
The tendency toward mass action must not be allowed to destroy
the sense of personal responsibility.
The basic problems of our times are still spiritual problems.

QUESTIONS AND DISCUSSION TOPICS

1. How do our times emphasize the moral responsibility of
every man?
2. How may the insights of science reinforce the insights of
religion? Discuss the need of the church and the university
for each other.
3. Discuss the importance of face-to-face relationships as a
force in moral achievement. How may such relationships be
promoted on a high level?
4. What gives meaning to life? Discuss the special need for
worship in such a day as ours.

5. How does our modern way of life tend to obscure individual responsibility? How may this be overcome?
6. How has our modern life put greater emphasis on the social consequences of sin? Does this mean that we ought to be less careful about personal transgressions?
7. In what sense are we "under moral obligation to see that the conditions of progress are met"? What does this involve?
8. How should we regard the profit motive in our modern world? What factors tend to make it a sound motive? What tend to make it unsound?
9. What are the two types of primary instincts? What is the importance of each? In what way may self-interest be a sound moral motive?
10. Discuss the modern cult of conformity. What are its advantages? Its disadvantages?
11. What insights as to the purpose of God in us are in special need of clarification in our modern age? How shall we do this?

THE HUMAN PREDICAMENT

Lesson 18

(Chapter 17, pp. 136-143)

LESSON PURPOSE

To show man's inescapable need of God and the inadequacy of the substitutes for obedience

POINTS TO EMPHASIZE

The importance of conscience and its inadequacy by itself
The importance of law-keeping and its inadequacy by itself
The importance of good works and their inadequacy of themselves
Our need of grace

QUESTIONS AND DISCUSSION TOPICS

1. What is the function of conscience?
2. Why must we be careful not to equate conscience with the voice of God?

248

3. Do you agree that "conscience must always be obeyed" and that "even an erring conscience should be obeyed"? Why? Under what conditions is conscience a safe guide for life?
4. What limitations of law-keeping are shown in the attitude of the rich young ruler who came to Jesus?
5. Discuss the statement of the text that "Even the most faithful obedience to the requirements of even the most enlightened legal system can never cure the world's ills." Do you agree? Why?
6. What is the relation of faith and works? Why are good works inadequate to fulfill the purpose of God in us?
7. How may cultural achievements help us to fulfill more perfectly the purpose of God in our creation? How may they become a barrier to this fulfillment?
8. Discuss the unbalance of the works of an ungodly man as mentioned in the text.
9. What can man do for man? What are the limits of what he can do for himself and his fellows?
10. What does God do for man, which man cannot do for himself, in terms of his conscience, his obedience to law, his good works?

THE HUMAN PREDICAMENT

Lesson 19, Part II Review

(Chapters 12-17)

LESSON PURPOSE

To review the major emphases of this section, with special attention given to the meaning and importance of the doctrine of agency

METHOD

Selected topics from the following list may be assigned to members of the class sometime in advance of the review, with instructions to be prepared to lead brief discussions of these topics.

Or it may be preferred to take a cross section of what has been discussed, making similar assignments.

DISCUSSION TOPICS
The nature of human freedom
Agency and sin
The significance of the doctrine of original sin
Your sins and mine
✕ Agency in the modern world
Our human predicament

ALTERNATE DISCUSSION TOPICS
The limitations and responsibilities of human freedom
The meaning of agency
✕ The inseparable connection of agency and responsibility
The social roots of sin
The social consequences of sin
The moral demands of our present world
Man's inability to save himself
Stewardship and the fulfillment of the divine purpose in us

REDEEMING LOVE

Lesson 20

(Chapter 18, pp. 146-152)

LESSON PURPOSE

To set forth the wonder of the love of God and the place of
love in our redemption

POINTS OF EMPHASIS

God is love. His love is not a phase of his life, but a fundamental aspect of the divine nature.

Out of love God takes the initiative for our redemption.

We come to know God as we come to know the Lord Jesus
Christ, especially in terms of his redemptive ministry.

We can do this effectively only as we are under the guidance
of the Holy Spirit.

QUESTIONS AND DISCUSSION TOPICS

1. Discuss the meaning of the statement that the word "sin" is
meaningful only in the context of faith in God.

250

2. Name some of the evidences that God has taken the initiative for our redemption. Can some of this be found in the nature of our creation?
3. The text states that "God wants us infinitely more than we want him." Do you agree? Why? What difference does your agreement or disagreement make?
4. Why was Jesus so basically opposed to sin? He has been called "the greatest of the revolutionaries." In what sense is this true?
5. How has Jesus enlarged your understanding of the love of God? Where have you seen this love manifest?
6. How are the ministries of the Father and the Son and the Holy Spirit related?
7. What are the major conditions of spiritual enlightenment?
8. What do we mean by the love of God, an emotional attitude? a protective attitude? a stimulating attitude? a paternal attitude? a sacrificial attitude?
9. In what way does the love of God put us under moral obligations? What does this have to do with our redemption from sin? What does it have to do with the fulfillment of the divine purpose in us?

CREATIVE FORGIVENESS

Lesson 21

(Chapter 19, pp. 153-160)

LESSON PURPOSE

To consider the nature of creative forgiveness with a view to better understanding of how it promotes the fulfillment of the divine purpose in us

POINTS TO EMPHASIZE

Forgiveness is a personal matter. Its problems are the problems of values and relationships.

Forgiveness is costly, both to the forgiver and the forgiven.

True forgiveness is only achieved as the forgiven comes to share in the forgiving spirit.

Forgiveness can change the significance of all that has happened.

251

QUESTIONS AND DISCUSSION TOPICS

1. What do we mean when we say that "The Christian solution for the problem of sin centers in forgiveness"?
2. How do you define forgiveness? What is the difference between forgiveness and the cancellation of a debt? Or the overlooking of an injury? How does love enter into forgiveness on the part of God? on the part of man?
3. How is intelligence involved in true forgiveness? What of patience? What of self-discipline?
4. Name some sinners whose lives were changed under the influence of Christ. What was the key factor in their salvation?
5. The apostle Paul says that "Where sin abounded, grace did much more abound." Comment on this with illustrations from the New Testament, the Book of Mormon, and church history.
6. Why does our heavenly Father require that we shall be forgiving as a condition of his forgiveness? Does our forgiving attitude have to precede our being forgiven, or is it an aspect of being forgiven?
7. In what way does a change in attitude on the part of a sinner affect the significance of his sins? In what sense is it true that "the future has yet to decide what past sins shall mean"?
8. Discuss the relation between divine forgiveness and the fulfillment of the divine purpose in us.

THE DIVINE ELEMENT IN FORGIVENESS

Lesson 22

(Chapter 20, pp. 161-168)

LESSON PURPOSE

To evoke a greater appreciation of the significance of the sacrifice of Christ at Calvary

POINTS TO EMPHASIZE

The need for God to take the initiative for our redemption
The bearing of divine love and wisdom on our forgiveness
The love manifest in the offering of Christ on Calvary
The appeal of Calvary to the best in men

252

1. Discuss the significance of the statement that "Forgiveness requires clear thought and deep personal involvement." Look for illustrations in life or literature.
2. Contrast human love and divine love. Why is human love inadequate to meet the problem of man's sinfulness?
3. Why did so many of the Jews resent the preaching of Jesus? Is similar preaching likely to meet similar resentment in our day? How may this be overcome?
4. The text states that "The cross carries the meaning which Jesus gave it—it speaks his message, not the message of his enemies." What is the evidence for this? Can men of Christlike temper of mind use the wickedness of men in similar fashion? How?
5. It took sacrificial courage for Jesus to follow his purpose through to the end at Calvary. What else did it take? What lessons are there here for us?
6. Tell in your own words what Calvary means to you.
7. How long does Calvary continue for God? Where a wise man loves sinners is it possible for him to avoid coming under the burden of the cross? Why?
8. Discuss the meaning of such scriptural expressions as "crucify Christ afresh," "crucified with him," "the fellowship of his sufferings."
9. Discuss the meaning of the statement that "No one who has known the love manifested at Calvary can ever again think too highly of himself, his possessions, or his ease."
10. In what way is the divine purpose in us made more clear in the light of what happened at Calvary?

FAITH AND FORGIVENESS

Lesson 23

(Chapter 21, pp. 169-176)

LESSON PURPOSE

To consider faith as the response to the love of God, especially as this was shown at Calvary, and to note its relation to forgiveness

The distinction between sins and sin
The nature of faith
Faith as the foundation for forgiveness
Justification by faith

QUESTIONS AND DISCUSSION TOPICS

1. Note the distinction in the text between "sin" and "sins." Why is this distinction important? Which is the more difficult to overcome?

2. Why should we trust Christ, who lived so long ago, to provide spiritual leadership in such a day as ours?

3. Discuss the statement of the text that "The greatest expression of atheism today is . . . unwillingness to commit our lives to God's purpose."

4. Discuss faith as an adventure of the spirit; as a declaration of dependence; as a vow of allegiance.

5. In what way does faith lead us to accept the divine verdict in our lives, in contrast with our own past verdicts? In this connection consider the statement of Jesus, "If any man will come after me, let him *deny himself.*"

6. How may a "temporary faith" or a "shallow faith" be dangerous? Which is more spiritually significant—the faith to be healed of physical ills or the faith to serve despite such ills?

7. How is faith in God connected with high morality? Is uncertainty concerning some interpretations of the faith sufficient justification for lowering moral standards? Discuss the tendency to excuse moral lacks in terms of intellectual uncertainty.

8. How is faith related to forgiveness? Is creative forgiveness possible without faith? Why?

9. What do we mean by "justification by faith" and "justification by grace"?

10. How does faith in God enable us to discern and fulfill the divine purpose in us?

254

THE RESPONSE OF REPENTANCE

Lesson 24

(Chapter 22, pp. 177-185)

LESSON PURPOSE

To sound the call to sincere and searching repentance

POINTS TO EMPHASIZE

The moral demand for repentance
The inadequacy of mere repenting
The sanity of accepting responsibility for our actions
The necessity for divine guidance and strength

QUESTIONS AND DISCUSSION TOPICS

1. What is the meaning of repentance? Distinguish between faith and repentance.

2. Discuss, briefly, the statement that "In true repentance we take God's part against ourselves."

3. Distinguish between repentance and repenting. Why is the former more significant than the latter?

4. Discuss the modern tendency to excuse ourselves in sin. Is this so modern? Why do we do it?

5. Discuss the meaning of the phrase "that impenitence which masquerades in the garb of righteousness." Give illustrations of this.

6. Why is it essential to spiritual health that we shall accept responsibility for our sinning? Discuss the importance of prayer in helping us to face up to this responsibility.

7. Discuss the meaning of a niggardly attitude in making reparation for injustice. What does this indicate in terms of the spirit of the one making such reparation? What light does this throw on the relation between reparation and repentance?

8. How is repentance connected with the fulfillment of the divine purpose in us? Is there any way in which the necessity for repentance can be avoided?

CONVERSION AND THE NEW BIRTH

Lesson 25

(Chapter 23, pp. 186-192)

To consider the importance of the experience of conversion or the new birth, noting that the outward evidences of this change are of secondary importance as compared with the change itself

POINTS TO EMPHASIZE

We need to explore the meaning of conversion and the new birth.

This is not an intellectual or an emotional experience, but an experience of the whole person.

Its significance is in its affirmations: that it is toward God rather than just away from sin.

The rate or the drama of conversion is of secondary importance to the depth and the reality of the experience.

QUESTIONS AND DISCUSSION TOPICS

1. The text affirms that a human being who lacks a central reason for existence is "not a man but a walking civil war." Illustrate this.

Red 2. What do we mean by conversion? Why is it required that conversion shall involve the whole man?

3. Contrast the affirmative and negative aspects of conversion. Do you agree that "without love there is no conversion"?

4. Name some persons mentioned in the scriptures who were soundly converted in movingly dramatic fashion. How do you account for their conversion?

5. Name some mentioned in the scriptures, or others, who have been soundly converted, but who seem to have come to their decision gradually and even reluctantly. Is there any reason to doubt the value of their conversion as compared with those coming to their decision more quickly?

6. Discuss the meaning of the term "new birth." Contrast it with "conversion."

7. The text says that "Like conversion, the new birth stands in sharp contrast with any scheme of cultural or moral reform." Discuss this. Is it sound?

8. Discuss the "explosive power of a new affection" in terms of the importance of conversion and the new birth.

256

BAPTISM AND THE DIVINE PURPOSE

Lesson 26

(Chapter 24, pp. 193-201)

To study the need for baptism and its relation to the achievement of the divine purpose in us

POINTS TO EMPHASIZE

The importance of membership in a spiritual community
The need for specific commitment
The social significance of baptism
The present need for such commitment

QUESTIONS AND DISCUSSION TOPICS

1. Discuss the meaning of the expression "a people." In what way is "a people" more than an association of individuals? In what sense do the disciples constitute a "peculiar people"?

2. The text comments that a "new birth is . . . more than an individual experience. It is a great event in the life of the family of God." Do you agree? Illustrate your answer.

3. Why was baptism important for the repentant Jews at Pentecost? What did it do for them?

4. In what way was the repentance to which Peter called more than "godly sorrow"? Are we justified in saying that it was "repentance unto life"? Why did Peter's concern over their repentance lead to his invitation to baptism?

5. Discuss the situation of the believer who is not baptized. Note how his repentance falls short of full effectiveness. Is it possible to escape the responsibility for enlistment which goes with enlightenment?

6. Why is it important that the new birth shall be symbolized in a physical act? Discuss the adequacy of baptism by immersion in water at the hands of one having authority as a symbol and an epitome of entrance into the life of the people of God.

7. Discuss the statement that "Men are saved by baptism as truly as by faith and repentance."

8. Discuss baptism as an act of humility, as a landmark of dedication, as a proclamation of faith, as a sequence of repentance, as a response of love.

9. What contribution does baptism make to the fulfillment of the divine purpose in us?

THE SPIRIT OF LIFE

Lesson 27

(Chapter 25, pp. 202-210)

LESSON PURPOSE

To renew our grateful awareness of our dependence on the Spirit of God in our attempt to fulfill the divine purpose in us

POINTS TO EMPHASIZE

The importance of sharing the Spirit of God among the people of God

The significance of the endowment in terms of light and power

The renewal of the Spirit in the Communion service and in the experience of communion

The constant availability of the Spirit

QUESTIONS AND DISCUSSION TOPICS

1. With what equipment did the early disciples begin their ministerial tasks? What was the most significant part of this equipment?

2. In harmony with the promise of the Lord Jesus the Spirit came to the disciples as their Guide and Comforter. How did the Spirit function as a "Comforter"?

3. To what degree does the body depend on the spirit which animates it? With this in mind, discuss the close connection between baptism and confirmation. How does the Spirit *confirm* the faithful?

4. What was the real significance of the endowment of the Holy Spirit among the early Christians? What is it today?

5. Discuss the joy of the saints as a gift of the Holy Spirit. Do we experience the richness of this joy as fully as we should? How may we enter more fully into the "joy unspeakable and full of glory" referred to by Peter?

6. Discuss the significance of the Holy Spirit as the spirit of victory.

7. Discuss the Communion as a "rite of remembrance and renewal." Discuss the relation of Communion and forgiveness and the Holy Spirit. How do bread and wine minister to these realities?

8. What are the characteristics of the life of a genuinely "spiritual" man?

9. How does the endowment of the Spirit of God enable us to see the divine purpose in us more clearly and to respond to it more fully?

258

A PROPHETIC PEOPLE

Lesson 28

(Chapter 26, pp. 211-219)

LESSON PURPOSE

To explore the meaning of our call to be a prophetic people

POINTS TO EMPHASIZE

Prophetic ministry is born of the Spirit and understood by that same Spirit.

There is a permanent quality in genuinely prophetic ministry.

The people of God are called to be a prophetic people.

Demands are made of spiritual maturity.

QUESTIONS AND DISCUSSION TOPICS

1. How are prophets called? What is the evidence of their calling? How do they prove their message? How do we know that it is true?

2. It has been said that the prophets "did not see different things, but saw things differently." Comment on this in the light of the text. In what did their clear vision center?

3. The prophets speak to men of all times. Why? What was the sound moral basis for life which they proclaimed? Discuss our present need for prophetic guidance.

4. In what sense was the Lord Jesus Christ the greatest of the prophets? Why do we interpret the work of other prophets in the light of his life and ministry?

5. How do we know the greatness of the Lord Jesus Christ? Discuss the work of the Spirit in relation to the ministry of the Savior.

6. What was the attitude of Moses toward the wide distribution of the spirit of prophecy? What was the expectation of Joel in this connection? What do we mean by the statement that "It is the will and purpose of God that his people shall be a prophetic people"?

7. Discuss the relation of integrity to spirituality. Is inclusive integrity possible to men who do not believe in God? Why?

8. Discuss and illustrate the emotional depth and maturity exhibited by a genuinely prophetic people. Discuss the need for *sustained* and *disciplined* indignation.

9. What should be the attitude of a prophetic people toward widely heralded causes? What is the relation of such causes to the cause of Zion?

259

10. What should be the attitude of a prophetic people toward education, research, philosophy? Why?
11. What is the inclusive task of a prophetic people in our generation?

THE CHRISTIAN HOPE

Lesson 29

(Chapter 27, pp. 220-225)

LESSON PURPOSE

To find challenge and courage in considering the Christian hope and the fact that this centers in God, in whom we have the best of all reasons to center our trust

POINTS TO EMPHASIZE

Hope faces the facts of life.

There are victories for those who "endure as seeing the invisible."

Hope centers in the achievement of the divine purpose in us, and pays the price of this achievement in faith.

Our hope is in God.

QUESTIONS AND DISCUSSION TOPICS

1. Discuss the relation of faith and hope. Give place in your discussion to the statement of the text that hope "is born of the Spirit's grip on ultimate realities."
2. Enumerate some of the disturbing facts which hope faces. How can we hope in view of such facts?
3. What is the final ground of Christian hope? For what may we hope in view of the nature of the guarantees of God?
4. Consider the resurrection of the Lord Jesus Christ in relation to the Christian hope. Consider the bearing of the doctrine of immortality and eternal life on the Christian hope.
5. Discuss hope as an essential part of the heroic man's equipment. To what type of "foolishness" is the Christian hope related? Why?
6. Discuss the statement of the text that our hope "is not in having our own way, but in God who has his loving way in us."
7. Does the Christian hope depend on avoidance of responsibility and suffering? on the perfection of our outward circumstances? on the rapid achievement of our good desires?
8. Since evil seems to be so well entrenched, why is despair so ungodly?

260

9. How may the purpose of God be achieved while our agency is recognized and respected? In what sense is God Lord of life?

10. How does our Christian hope minister to the achievement of the divine purpose in us?

THE WAY OF REDEMPTION

Lesson 30, Part III Review

(Chapters   18-27)

LESSON PURPOSE

To review the major emphases of this section, with special concern for the means of redemption provided by the grace of God.

METHOD

Selected topics from the following list may be assigned to members of the class some time in advance of the review, with instructions to be prepared to lead brief discussions of these topics.

Or it may be found preferable to take a cross section of what has been discussed, making assignments in a similar fashion.

DISCUSSION TOPICS

The redemptive character of divine love
Creative forgiveness
The divine contribution in forgiveness
Faith and forgiveness
The response of repentance
Conversion and the new birth   *Feb 21*
The significance of baptism
The Spirit of God, which is the Spirit of Life
A prophetic people
The Christian hope

ALTERNATE DISCUSSION TOPICS

The divine initiative for our redemption
The demands of forgiveness
The meaning of the cross in Christian experience
The necessity of faith
The sanity of repentance
The meaning of conversion
The social significance of baptism
The spirit of the New Order
The demands of spiritual maturity
Christ in you, the hope of glory

261